EVERYTHING
WAS GREAT

UNTIL IT SUCKED

Lazy Fascist Press
An Imprint of Eraserhead Press

Eraserhead Press
c/o Lazy Fascist
205 NE Bryant Street
Portland, OR 97211

WWW.LAZYFASCISTPRESS.COM

ISBN: 978-1-62105-064-3

Cover photos by Leah Wensink

Cover design by Matthew Revert

Cover Model: Patrick Wensink

Facts can be hazy. These essays are true to the best knowledge of the author.

Printed in the USA.

EVERYTHING WAS GREAT UNTIL IT SUCKED

One Man's Journey from Fake IDs and BBQ Sauce
Sales to Stay-at-Home-Dad and Bestselling Author

ESSAYS BY
PATRICK WENSINK

LAZY FASCIST PRESS
PORTLAND, OREGON

TABLE OF CONTENTS

To Ryan Miller,
my favorite storyteller.

THE SEAFOOD DIET:
AN INTRODUCTION TO THIS BOOK

I've never known an American economy that didn't smell like Red Lobster's dumpster.

In 2002, the job market essentially died right around the time I graduated college. About the time I was first on my own. Experts told us: "Things will turn around any month now."

Today's graduates know what they're getting into. They've been watching this sunken ship we call an economy for half their lives. But, a decade ago I was on the observation deck playing shuffle board when it started to take on water. "Any month now," the captain told thousands of people like me. "We'll start floating again."

That, of course, never happened. Over the years we stopped pointing fingers at terrorists for this mess and started blaming everyone from Wall Street brokers, to mortgage bankers, to the ever-fickle chinchilla trade.

Instead of living the post-college American dream of landing a stable job and owning a riding lawnmower, I did…let's just say… *other stuff*. Assembling this essay collection, I realized these stories are sewn together by folks like me who were involuntarily bucked from the status quo. This book is populated by American gymnastic heroes shilling for Phizer, anarchist clowns doing unspeakable acts just to cover the rent and clueless neighbor boys getting creative with the marijuana trade. Me, I failed and failed and failed at life.

Inadvertently, *Everything Was Great Until it Sucked* is an account of being the first generation to enter the workforce during this recession. It's a close-up shot of people like me who had no choice but to laugh as the ship's water rose to our waist, then our chest, then our nose. This book is about our frustration and disappointment in a rapidly sinking world we were constantly promised would improve any month now.

These essays, ranging from emails to friends to humor pieces in *The Huffington Post,* illuminate a life that wouldn't have been possible if experts' magic month ever arrived. I'm not saying this economic Titanic is a good thing. I'm just saying it created paths we wouldn't have dared walk otherwise.

Any month now.

Any month now.

Any month now.

-Patrick Wensink

105,000 EPISODES OF *ALF* CAN'T BE WRONG

History's shortest marriage spanned little more than 30 minutes. According to *Europe News,* a Turkish man and a Greek woman couldn't last longer than an episode of *Alf* before they got their lawyers on the phone. In their defense, those two nations hate each other the way I hated vegetables as a boy. Common sense says ouzo and double-dares had more than a little to do with those nuptials.

By comparison, I have been married for almost six years. But also if not for booze, the two of us wouldn't have lasted beyond *Alf's* first commercial break.

More directly, Leah and I owe it all to bad fake IDs.

We were 19 on our first date and things couldn't have gone worse. I suggested taking her to the classiest, most romantic establishment I could think of. Olive Garden. I was so nervous, I forget my wallet.

Leah graciously paid for our entire meal.

"Let's go to Flanagan's," I said on the car ride home, hoping to make up for her fettuccine charity act. I wanted to repay her: "Drinks are on me!"

We went back to my dorm room, grabbed my wallet and were off to the bar. Flanagan's was an Irish pub in name only. Its décor was less polished cherry wood and more late-century bomb shelter. Lighting came courtesy of Milwaukee's Best, not stained glass lampshades.

Christmas break began that day, so the place was dead. Normally, the small room was packed four people deep at the bar. On an average Thursday evening folks waved money at the bartender like there was a cockfight behind the beer taps. But that night, maybe three people lined up outside and empty tables were spread throughout.

"ID?" the door man in a tight black shirt and way too much aftershave said. His nametag read: Brad.

Leah handed hers over. It said she was "Dawn" and was 26. It was an actual driver's license passed down from sorority sister to sorority sister like an heirloom.

My ID was not so convincing. It had no honest lineage like Dawn. I was supposedly Terry M. Dover, age 21.

As my byline shows, I am not Terry M. Dover. Terry was born in a fashion that looks absolutely ancient now. I might as well have been chiseling Terry's name into granite. Remember, it was the late 90s, IDs didn't have those pesky scannable backsides. Terry M. Dover slid into my wallet as a result of some *Day of the Jackal*-type ingenuity, now-archaic computer software and several cases of domestic light beer.

"ID?" Brad asked.

I opened my wallet and flashed my handsome face. Unlike Dawn, Terry was actually a picture of me.

Confident that this sold the door man, I stepped toward Flanagan's neon-lit guts, ready to repair the Olive Garden's damage. The punch of stale beer was heavy in the air. My mind calculated ways to repair my suppertime snafu. It was time to turn on the old Terry M. Dover charm!

The bouncer held out a meaty arm. "Take it out of your wallet, please," he instructed, rising from his stool. Brad was tall with arms like truck tires.

Oh shit.

Terry M. Dover was never to be removed from the wallet. Never. That was a no-no. Letting Terry see daylight was suicide.

"This is a fake ID," Brad the bouncer said, flipping it over a few times in his thick fingers.

Panic pulled me down with wicked gravity. First the Olive Garden mess, now this! Terry M. Dover was harakiri for my love life. I was never much of a hotshot with the XX chromosome set in high school. College hadn't been much better. Now I was disemboweling a golden opportunity with this beautiful girl, *twice*, thanks to my ineptitude. She would probably stay at the bar, meet some stranger, marry him, have his kids, they'd file their taxes jointly! Clearly, she would never speak to me again.

Defeated, I settled for the truth. "Yeah," I said. "Yeah, it is."

Mister Thick Arms held Terry up to the light, angled it and found no hologram.

Then I realized I could get in trouble. Go to court. Be fined. Jailed. Fake IDs were illegal. This guy could've been an off-duty cop. And there, smelling the cigarette smoke from a table of frat guys, my guts dropped into an uncharted Eighth Circle of Hell. One reserved for idiot lawbreakers and wallet-forgetters trying to impress a girl.

"How'd you make it?" Brad said, curious.

"Well, you know what Photoshop is?" Remember this was the 90s. Most people had Lycos email addresses, for God's sake.

"Uh huh."

"My buddy, Medved, scanned a real person's ID, then Photoshopped my picture into it. Then we airbrushed the address out and filled it in with *that*." I said, pointing to Terry Dover's make-believe address on Beane Boulevard.

"Okay, but this is a real ID," he said, flicking the license. "Plastic."

The bouncer was roasting me over coals. Ripping out my fingernails before the decapitation. By now Leah had turned around to find her date delayed. She approached the entrance with confusion and disappointment on her face.

"We took my original ID and erased the front with nail polish remover."

"Really?"

"Yeah. Then we just printed off the Photoshop ID on good paper and laminated it onto the plastic. Then we used pencil erasers to scuff up the front and make it look worn."

"And this thing works?"

"Belmont Liquors lets me buy beer." Ooops, I thought. Shit. Well, there goes that connection. Nice work not telling a lie, George Washington.

"Huh," Brad said, holding my romantic life in his fingers. "It's pretty good."

"Uh, thanks?"

"Go have fun." He looked over my shoulder. "Next."

I wasn't drunk when I stepped across Flanagan's sticky tile floor, but I felt it. Every nerve electric zapped into the next.

I repaid Leah in drinks.

We *did* have fun, Brad.

We started dating. We got married. We filed our taxes jointly. We had a son. And it was all thanks to Brad the bouncer. And probably also thanks to the fact that we are neither Turkish or Greek.

As of this writing, Leah and I have been together the length of 105,000 *Alf* episodes.

Cheers, Brad!

TEETH. WHAT A PAIN IN THE ASS

Teeth. What a pain in the ass.

Once in a while you just wish someone would do you a favor and punch them out of your mouth.

Not recently, though. My last trip to the dentist was actually a success. This was my first visit to a new office and I was a little scared because the folks in charge are Doctor Payne and Doctor Rackett. It's like the punch line to a joke or the door of a law firm in a Bugs Bunny cartoon—Dewy, Cheatem & Howe. In spite of the intimidating namesake, they turned out to be an amiable bunch and provided the fantastic news that my mouth was cavity-free. I feel like the Pope missing a sniper's bullet every time my teeth get a clean bill of health.

Probably because I've had my share of cavities.

See, my childhood Pepsi intake was legendary. I'm pretty sure I was so caffeinated that, at one point, I didn't sleep during 1988. Needless to say, my cavity bill helped my dentist's kids go Ivy League.

Like how some families are all democrats or Yankees fans, we were strictly a Pepsi house. Not because it tasted superior to other bubbly brown beverages, but because my dad worked at a soda can factory. A factory that did not manufacture Coke cans. So, it was an unspoken rule that we couldn't give the *other guys* our business and potentially put dad out of work. That'd be like buying war bonds from Hitler.

Thankfully, the soda can factory provided good dental insurance. Over the years I needed it. I had so much enamel repaired I grew a little envious of my grandma. She had dentures. Removable teeth that never get cavities? Sign me up, I thought. This was the same corner of my brain that hoped I'd go prematurely bald because combing my hair every morning was becoming a real nuisance.

I begged and begged to be the first kid on my block with dentures but, of course, my parents declined. And so the fillings continued. You'd think Doctor Spragg suspected there was oil in my teeth as often as he drilled. I wouldn't have put it past him to construct an oil derrick in my head. The Doc hated children. He tormented us—finding the longest Novocain needles in Northwest Ohio and "cleaning" our teeth for maximum blood loss. I'm sure he was sad when the only gusher sprung up red, not crude oil black.

But dad seemed to get along with Doctor Spragg, so I went twice a year for checkups and endless fillings. He and I became a regular Batman and Joker. After the dental assistant's exam, he'd mosey in a half-hour to an hour later, just to make me sweat. He was pink-skinned and packing weight onto a once-thin face. He wore heavy glasses and spoke with a voice I can't forget. Nothing extravagant: calm, blunt, monotone. The doctor always talked down to kids, as if nobody ever informed us about the importance of flossing or how sugary drinks were bad news.

Little did Dr. Spragg know I was guzzling Pepsi to keep dad afloat, which led to cavities, which kept Dr. Spragg afloat. I was an important cog in the business cycle! The entire economy of Northwest Ohio depended on me drinking three, four or even five cans of soda a day.

Spragg didn't seem to agree that my pop consumption was so crucial. Actually, I doubt he was ever really listening in the first place. The man not only detested kids, but barely noticed they were in the chair. However, I got his attention one sweet day when I was 13.

Though my molars mimicked Manhattan potholes, their alignment wasn't too shabby. My smile was pretty straight, save for one pesky incisor that looked pushed-in. If my teeth went to school, the majority were summa cum laude, but that incisor rode the short bus. He kind of slouched back, afraid to stand in line with the rest of the class.

Batman and Joker battled over the subject of braces for years. Doctor Spragg would practically bore me to sleep with that condescending voice: "Patrick, I think we'd better take care of your alignment. You *need* braces. It's a pretty simple procedure."

And I would respond, always, with: "No thanks. I'm happy the way things are."

Six months later, we'd spar again. Like a married couple, we settled into a happy rut. That is, until I was 13 and the Joker tired of Batman's moral victories.

"Patrick, that incisor is a problem. Not to mention your canine is causing a shift in your molars. And on top of that, you're medulla oblongata is playing heck with your third metacarpal."

I was no tooth wiz, but something told me he was just making things up to create a pile.

"No thanks," I smiled crooked. "I love me just the way I am."

"I don't think this is a decision *you* should be making." His voice rose up from the monotone swamp with a fiery thrust. Some rocket of dental dominance had been launched my way. The cold war of braces was reaching Cuban Missile Crisis levels. His finger was on the red button. "Braces are a decision your parents should make for you. You don't have a say in this."

"I don't have a say in my own teeth?"

"No. Who drove you here today?"

"My mom."

"Good. Sit tight." And he was off to the waiting room. The entire time I was calling him names from R-rated movies I had snuck in at the time. These words were fresh and vulgar and couldn't do justice toward the underhanded stunt Spragg just pulled.

This man was becoming a threat to my childhood happiness. Braces would have doomed me at that age. I was already awkward, pimply and not exactly Cary Grant with the ladies. Braces would have undoubtedly killed my social life. I might as well have shown up to school wearing a gingham dress.

Mom quickly returned with the evil doctor. He explained how my incisor was misbehaving and how my patella and phalanges were butting against my molars and, yes, there still was a decent chance of oil being discovered in my head.

"So, I told Patrick, this is a decision your mother should make. Braces are very important to oral health and appearances," Spragg said. "He understands how crucial this is. I have to recommend braces. Wouldn't you agree, Mrs. Wensink?"

Mom looked at the doctor. Then she looked at me.

My head was still swirling with obscenities and replaying his line, "*You don't have a say in this… You don't have a say in this…*"

And then, at the zero hour, my mouth was saved. Mom made a little squint back at Spragg, like he spoke another language. "I don't know. They're his teeth. He can do whatever he wants. If Patrick doesn't want braces that's fine with me."

Fireworks went off in my head. A Macy's parade was held in Mom's honor up there, too. Free cake and ice cream and gallons of Pepsi for all! Somehow, I'd won this leg of the Cold War. Not only that, but victory came in just about the sweetest way possible: Spragg failed to outfox me by using my own mother.

Ahhh, but Spragg would have his revenge. Like any good super-villain, he might lose a battle, but he never forgot.

Fast forward eight years, I was in college and America's economy resembled a chemical toilet. My parents—knowing the likelihood of their son landing a job with dental benefits was unlikely—suggested I get my wisdom teeth pulled before I was dropped from the family insurance after graduation. Spragg had been mentioning my wisdom teeth were getting pretty ripe and, while there was no pain, it'd be a good idea to get this preemptively taken care of.

For once, I took his advice and volunteered for wisdom tooth removal. Most people I knew had painful stories about their back teeth clawing from their jaw. No thanks. Plus, I was very curious about nitrous oxide. For every story of excruciating wisdom tooth horror, I'd heard miracle tales of sucking on a facemask, counting backward from 10 and having dreams fit for Alice in Wonderland. That sounded alright to me. Doctor Spragg, you and I might just get to be friends yet, I thought.

As the assistants prepped me, they were surprised by how calm I was, smiling and joking. I felt like a million bucks.

And then he entered the room and gave some tense-lipped small talk. Keep your friends close, but your enemies closer, ay, Spragg? "Okay," he told his assistant. "I'll need the Novocain now." He held a painkilling needle fit for a brontosaurus.

My head spun a little, but not in the LSD-like ride I was hoping with the gas. It was the panicked sensation of dreams being choked. Suddenly, my life was also resembling a chemical toilet.

"Hold on," I said. "Where's the gas?"

"I don't believe in gas," the doctor said, finger-tapping this javelin he called a syringe.

"Well, *I* believe in gas. I want to be knocked out."

Doctor Spragg's dopey eyes lit up. His voice dropped and I swore it picked up a fiendish echo, like he was speaking in some granite cathedral. "We don't have any nitrous oxide, even if you did want some. I strictly use Novocain for these procedures." A grin formed atop his rosacea-plagued cheeks. "You'll thank me for this. You'll be more lucid afterward. You can even drive yourself home. Can't do that with the gas."

"My mom is picking me up. I don't need to drive. I want the gas."

The doctor chuckled a little, held that Novocain spear and growled, "open wide."

What followed were the most hellish couple hours imaginable. I should have known he would inflict maximum pain when, as he jammed the needle into my gums, he sort of hummed under his breath: "Will you look at that. Your alignment is a little off. You sure could use braces."

You son of a bitch! Blazed flaming letters across my mind.

From there I realized why most humane doctors knock patients out. Sure, wisdom tooth removal is painful, but that's not the worst of it. Just like people don't want to see where veal cutlets come from, folks don't want to know the slasher movie playing inside their mouth during a tooth extraction.

Doctor Spragg didn't fill me in on what specific torture they were up to, but there was a lot of drilling and a noxious smell of burning enamel, which wasn't unlike burnt hair or scorched flesh. This, I assumed, was just prep work, because Doctor Doom pulled out a little crowbar-like device and locked it to a wisdom tooth, stretching my jaw wide. Spragg began prying at my tooth like a stubborn roofing nail. Cracking sounds filled the air and earthquake vibrations tremored through my body.

This repeated three times. Luckily, I only had a trio of wisdom teeth and not the usual fourth.

I was so furious about being denied gas, I don't remember how we parted ways. The R-rated obscenities I used at 13 were nothing compared to the encyclopedia of fury that a few years of college English classes built. Finally, my mouth was packed full of gauze and I was told to take aspirin. Not even some sweet prescription painkillers.

Teeth. What a pain in the ass.

Revenge was best served with a mouthful of cotton wads. Spragg struck back and definitely hit me deep. I knew he was an underhanded adversary, but these were new depths.

One year later, we entered the final round of my adolescent dental boxing match. I was back in the dentist's chair under suspicious circumstances.

When I graduated from college, some friends and I took a road trip to Daytona Beach. For the first few days we enjoyed good times, binge drinking and sunburns. On the fourth night of our weeklong trip, one bar offered yard glasses of Red Bull and vodka. Best I can remember, I downed two of these tall drinks.

And then…nothing.

I was no stranger to drinking. My friends and I usually felt like we were doing something wrong on Friday and Saturday nights if we hadn't polished off a case of cheap beer before even going out for the evening. But this toxic combination of Russia's favorite liquor and meth-heads' preferred sugar buzz screwed something up inside me. My brain looked a lot like a television after someone held a magnet to the screen.

Blackout is too tame a word. I make a living thinking of words and I am coming up empty. All I know is that I woke up in my hotel room, surrounded by two of my best friends, Ben and Don, and my yellow T-shirt was wet with blood.

One tooth—that pesky incisor Doctor Spragg hated so much—was cracked. Shattered, to be exact. It felt like a knife blade rising from my gumline.

Apparently, my buddy, Ben, found me sleeping on the balcony. Fearing I would drunkenly take a four-story tumble, he tried coaxing me back to the room. I took offense and got so angry that the only sensible way Ben could keep this energy-drink-and-vodka-fueled animal at bay was to deck me in the mouth.

I do not question this logic. I am known to be a handful when drunk, though this was my first beating. It was deserved.

After a very silent 10 hour drive back to Ohio, I made an emergency appointment with Doctor Spragg. We touched gloves and came out swinging at the bell.

"How did you crack your tooth?" he asked, inspecting my open mouth.

"I fell off my bike," I said. I was, at the time, concerned that if I told the truth two things would happen:

1. Some strange insurance snafu might occur and force my pal (yes, we're still friends. This budding "Sugar" Ray Leonard was actually a groomsman in my wedding!) to pay for the dental work.

2. Pleased that someone landed the punch he'd been waiting to throw for years, Doctor Spragg might get up and dance.

"Strange. Your face looks fine. A person falls off his bike, I'd think they'd have cuts and scrapes and black eyes."

"Uh, yeah…freak chance."

"Yes. Freakish." And with that, he let the subject drop.

A rare sign of compassion. Was it possible Doc Spragg was once a stupid kid, making mistakes with his teeth? Or was he just lowering my defenses so he could claim the only way to fix this cracked tooth was thousands of dollars in braces? Did he now plan to ruin my early 20s instead of my teens?

The doc said I needed a crown and a root canal. He numbed me up with his precious Novocain and got to work.

The entire process wasn't too rough. Fast, even. And then clouds opened up above our little Batman/Joker boxing ring when I left the office. My girlfriend, who actually thought my crooked tooth was cute (suck on that, Spragg!) took a long look at my mouth. "Your teeth…"

"Is it that obvious?"

"No, you can't tell at all. Look how straight they are."

"What?"

"That one tooth that was always a little pushed in, it's in line with the others. It's like you got braces or something."

And she was right. My God, I thought, Spragg could have put that tooth right back into its old position, he could have dropped it further cockeyed, could have even turned it sideways. But no, he fixed it. He killed two birds with one stone.

Maybe three birds. Because, for the first time in my life, I saw it was possible to bury a hatchet for the greater good. He showed me you can dislike someone and still work with them. He showed me there is a grey area in life wide enough to land a plane on. A lesson which proved invaluable for the many, many random jobs I held afterward. No matter how badly I failed at them I had this nugget.

Was it possible that being punched in the mouth was the most positive thing that ever happened to me? Not only did I get a valuable lesson, but I avoided costly and embarrassing braces and clearly won the battle of wills with old Spragg. He couldn't keep fighting. This little incisor was his white flag.

And honestly, if you follow the thread of this one rogue tooth and me getting socked in the face, I even proved how smart I was to my parents. Not that my dad was right for liking Spragg or my mom was wrong for defending me against him. My smile was saved by fake teeth. Just like grandma. Looking back, I can only imagine how successful I would have been if mom and dad had agreed to fix me up with dentures like I'd asked in the first place.

Teeth. What a pain in the ass.

BENOCIDE

"Ugh," I say. The cement in my arteries thickens a little when I grab the mail. Tuesday is usually junk mail day and today's no different. There are always ads for pizza delivery and oil changes and car insurance. But there is also a glossy ad for Burger King.

Flashing through the ads I stop on this one. It looks like you'd expect: there are flames and cheese and meat and sesame seed buns. But for the first time, I'm counting while looking at a hamburger.

"Holy shit, Leah," I yell into the kitchen. "Come look at this." I usually save this level of excitement for adorable kitties wandering onto the porch or strange growths on my neck, but this is a heart-stopper.

I've always assumed the fast food industry long ago reached its gluttony plateau. Someone in a test kitchen came up with the Big Mac and the Whopper and breathed a sigh of relief. For decades, two patties and a ton of vegetables was as close to the gastronomical abyss as anyone cared to go. Hell, they even shuffled in an extra slice of bread to show people they meant business.

But recently, our friend, the Burger King, has shattered that glass ceiling. The King fancies himself as Christopher Columbus. Where the rest of the restaurant industry has told him the world is flat, he says there is more out there. Limitless possibilities. His Nina, Pinta and Santa Maria of calories landed on my shore today in the form of a coupon.

"One...two..." I say, counting to make sure I'm not hallucinating. Even though I will never sit down and eat what I am counting, my heart sputters like our '88 Subaru. "Three...shit, I was right. Four!"

In a streak of overindulgence that could only happen in America, a country also in desperate need of five bladed disposable razors, Burger King shocks the beef-loving world with the "Quad."

This tower of digestive tract destruction is four cheeseburgers and a fistful of bacon between two sesame seed buns. Not a veggie in sight. (19-year-old me would have loved The Quad.) It's safe to assume our spare tire weighs less.

"God," my wife says. "That sounds like Ben-ocide."

I do some research online. The Burger King's court is tight-lipped and there is not a single mention of the Quad's nutritional information. So I make do by multiplying a bacon double cheeseburger by two.

The results nearly induce seizure.

Hypothetically, let's say you go to the doctor and she says: "Look, I'm not going to lie. Your heart is in bad shape. By my calculations if you ingest a thousand more calories today, you will die." And, just for argument's sake, let's say your life isn't going so smoothly. Your dog died, your wife is cheating on you and, well, your arteries are running on fumes. You decide it's time for assisted suicide.

Here is where your dilemma begins. You can either eat three-quarters of a bag of Oreos or a single Quad hamburger. Both lug equal artery arsenals. That, in case you aren't counting, is an exhausting amount of calories.

This little beef grenade will cripple American cholesterol counts. Like radiation, bacon grease will seep into our skin by getting close. Regardless, millions will eat it.

But why?

Because America always wins, that's why! Look at us, our razors have more blades, our hamburgers have more levels, hell, if it was useful we'd put more wheels on our cars. Only a Communist would follow the Surgeon General's suggested 2,000 calorie daily diet.

Nowhere is this more blindingly obvious than Texas, the home of Ben-ocide.

To learn more, we must roll back the clock about five years:

"Whoa, Free 72oz Steak Dinner," I say. "I like free steak."

I'm 21 and broke and in the middle of Texas. My three best friends and I are limping back to Ohio after a blurry week in Vegas. Spring break will be over soon and we need to get back to Dayton and sleep. We'll be graduating college soon. I have resumes to tighten and mail out.

Texas is huge and boring, but its panhandle looks like the business end of a coma. It's dead grass and flat land and billboards for hundreds of miles. Fortunately, some of these billboards advertise free steak.

"Whoa, there it is again," Ben, says. We whip by a black billboard with a tow truck-sized steak painted on it. This NY strip is juicy and brown and has shakes of pepper that could double as black softballs.

We put our heads together and decide that it's some type of redneck trap. Down a dirt road offering free beef is a Texas-sized bullring where they capture steak seekers and make us fight for our lives against angry steers.

Another few miles and this question is answered:
FREE 72oz Steak Dinner at the BIG TEXAN Steak Ranch. Amarillo, TX – 107 mi.

In awe, we push on through the heat and stink of West Texas. We don't even stop at the Cadillac Graveyard—a roadside attraction that looks like Stonehenge if the Druids worked for GM.

For 107 Miles we're hit with the promise of free meat every few minutes. As the message grinds further into our psyches someone, probably our pal, Don—since he's the smartest—reads the fine print. "It says, 'must eat entire meal,' did you guys see that?"

We didn't. Visions of porterhouses were dancing through our heads. The billboard repetition mutates my skull into a tender, pink filet.

Over an hour after our first promise of free beef, we roll into the Big Texan Steak Ranch. It's a cartoon—everything painted a headache-inducing shade of Day-Glo yellow and blue. The parking lot features more novelty chuck wagons than cars. This place should be the capitol building of Texas, we decide. The restaurant also boasts a motel with a pool shaped like Texas.

Unfazed, we head for the beef.

I'm knocked out cold by the interior. It looks like Ted Nugent's living room. Dead animals dangle from every inch of the raw wooden beams. The yellowing chandelier is nothing but pure antler. Every table is covered with black and white cowhide.

"Y'all here for the Big Texan?" a sparky waitress asks.

"Well," Medved, says. "What is that, exactly?"

"Here's the scoop, fellas," she says, flipping open the menu. "Ya gotta eat the seventy-two ounce steak, that's four-and-a-half pounds, give or take. Plus, a baked potato, salad, shrimp cocktail and dinner roll."

"H-how much?" I say.

We collectively swallow a four-and-a-half pound lump down our throats.

"Here's the catch," she smiles. "Gotta do it in under an hour."

"What if we don't finish?" Medved asks.

"Gotta pay fifty-nine-ninety-nine, plus tax."

"Whoa," Ben says. "We'll need to think this over."

We'd heard of such offers from movies like *The Great Outdoors* but never seen them up close [**Editor's Note:** This was 2002, back before cable TV was filled with restaurants and eating challenges]. Medved and I bail out immediately. We volunteer our services as eating coaches. The other guys sit around for a couple tense minutes. Hey, it's spring break, we say, why not? Next to *free sex*, no two words make a 21-year-old man's neck tingle like *free meat*.

"You two will never have this chance again. It would be un-American not to."

After some nudging from their coaches, Don and Ben agree to have an old-fashioned Lone Star State shootout.

Ben and Don order the biggie. Medved goes for the 12oz strip steak and I totally retreat and pick chicken. A few minutes later, our loudmouth waitress has some paperwork to sign. In essence, the waiver clears the Steak Ranch of any wrongdoing if the boys choke on gristle or get sent to the hospital with beef poisoning. (Widely known as the third most common type of poisoning in Texas.) But it's equal parts comforting and creepy to know the Big Texan takes eating, or at least choking, so seriously.

"How do you want it cooked?" the waitress asks.

"What do you recommend?" Don says.

"Well, usually medium. Once, this old farmer from down the road ate two in the hour. They were medium. And the record holder, this guy from the Cincinnati Reds, he ate the whole dinner in nine minutes. I think that was medium, too."

My gut blossoms with ulcers just imagining a guy in a gray and red uniform wolfing down six pounds of food in less time than it takes to finish an inning.

"Yep, he just chopped up the potato, the shrimp and the salad and rolled them into the steak like a burrito and worked away at it."

Still picturing this carnivore burrito supreme, our gladiators are rushed onto a stage in the middle of the dining room with a huge clock behind it.

"Ladies and gentlemen, can I have your attention," the hefty restaurant manager says. "We got Ben and Don here, all the way from Ohio, and they're gonna go for the Big Texan! Let's hear it for 'em."

The waitresses bring out the two largest bovine slices imaginable. Two brown couch cushions of steak surrounded by all the fixins.

The clock begins and the boys set to work. People stop eating to snap pictures like it's the circus. But this is better than the fire eater standing on the bearded lady's shoulders, juggling knives. This is real. It's some sort of modern bravery.

My buddies stare heart disease square in the eye without flinching. I proudly start taking pictures, too. It might be the last time we see them, I realize.

Half an hour into the feast, with their faces turning the same pink as the dead center of their steaks, I nudge Coach Medved: "Wanna take bets on who wins?"

Medved, a computer science major and notorious gambler, perks up: "Ben, totally."

"Bullshit," I say. "You're on. I got Donny."

Don plays rugby and is well known as an amateur competitive eater. He once, for $20, ate 12 of the hottest chicken wings Dayton, OH had to offer in less than two minutes. Don is a sure thing. Ben is skinny and known to occasionally eat salad.

"This is suicide," we mutter with glee

"No, it's Ben-ocide!"Medved says.

Ten minutes later, Don bows out. Three-quarters into the meal he stops. His pink fingers can't lift the fork. He's sweating Worcestershire. I'm crushed.

My horse was such a sure thing.

Coach Medved outfoxed me.

Sure, Don is a big eater, but he is also Pre-Med and has a head full of common sense. He knows victory will make him sick for at least a week and shave months, possibly years, off his life.

Ben, on the other hand, left all his money at the blackjack table in Vegas. He *literally* has no money. He can't pay for the meal if he loses, so he must finish. Plus, we've been prepping him for this moment the entire trip. Playing a game called "What Won't Ben Eat?"

The highlight was a week-old hotdog at a gas station in Kansas at 3AM. It was grey and looked like grandma's fingers. It crackled as he chewed. But Ben finished.

I should have seen this coming.

Forty-five minutes into the meal, Big Ben's plate is nothing but a puddle of blood. His face is round and red, as he puts his napkin on the table and is declared the Supreme Beef Master.

I'm so proud, my testosterone hits new highs.

Our waitress asks if he wants dessert. Without a second thought he says, "Cheesecake, please." He finishes that too. What a man.

Gleaming, Coach Medved and I roll our pals out the door. "So how was the steak?" he says.

What comes next is possibly the greatest quote ever spoken in my presence. I'm going to get this etched in Ben's tombstone when he dies, which shouldn't be long considering what his cholesterol must look like.

Ben: "The first three pounds were delicious!"

After a long session of stretching, lying on the hot Texas pavement and uncomfortable vomiting, we are back on the road toward home. Winners.

Even though I lost the bet, I'm really glad Ben won the steak eating championship. Inevitably, on some Tuesday in the future when I get my mail, I'll smile. It's only a matter of time before Burger King puts a five pound slab of steak between two sesame seed buns and calls it the "Ben-ocide." The "Don-ocide," doesn't have the same ring.

POVERTY + LONELINESS: A MATH LESSON

Poverty does strange things to men.

Some are brought closer together. Some are repelled by lack of cash. Some men will even, under extreme financial duress, sing karaoke for middle aged divorcees to save money.

This story is Tucson's fault, really.

The city did not welcome us with open arms. It embraced my college buddy, Ryan, and I with, at best, cactus arms—a painful Sonoran spirit.

We were living in a one bedroom apartment. Two foldable camping chairs for furniture. One mattress. We took turns on the used Sealy in the bedroom. If it was your night off, you slept on a leaky air mattress in the living room. Usually, you woke up flat on the carpet.

Even worse than our living arrangements were our financial futures and lack of new friends. Here's some quick math: **Poverty + Loneliness = Bad Times.**

Ryan and I moved to Arizona after graduation with bright plans of living some sort of beat poet lifestyle—minus the poetry. Lounging in hammocks. Cooking peyote stews. Wrestling coyotes.

We did not relocate to the desert for its solitude.

But that loneliness had no trouble finding our address.

A quick lesson for those not familiar with Tucson:

1. There are no trees to even hang hammocks from. Besides, it's 120 degrees outside, so who'd want to lay out? Summer in the Sonoran Desert is like winter everywhere else—nobody leaves the house.

2. We probably could have made peyote stew if we'd asked. But drugs scared us. We stuck to weird, cheap, domestic beers like Durango.

3. I once saw a coyote in the parking lot of a bar. It looked like a dirty dog. Wrestling it as some sort of spirit quest looked like a ticket to Rabies-Town.

As previously mentioned, friends were tough to make. Impossible. Tucson's population was around 500,000 and none of them wanted anything to do with two Midwestern nerds. We unsuccessfully tried making friends everywhere from rock concerts, to record shops, to hiking trails. Our girlfriends back East were still several months away from following us on this journey.

The city was mostly retirees and college kids. We were neither. What 20-somethings existed had lived in Tucson their entire life and didn't seem interested in meeting pale, overly-friendly dudes from Ohio who drank too much.

Ryan and I had just left college. The real world didn't make sense.

We were so naïve and used to school life, we didn't understand the weird looks people gave when we explained that we were just two "buddies" sharing a one bedroom apartment.

Ryan and I sat around that bleak, windowless apartment a lot. Drinking Durango. We listened to Kris Kristofferson repeatedly. We often wondered if a 2,000 mile move—with no secure jobs or savings—was such a terrific idea.

Ryan—mellow tempered, lanky and ginger-haired with a new biology degree—worked at a shop specializing in square bagels. His tenure as shift leader became a local legend when he let all the high school employees get high in the freezer.

Sitting on a Communications degree, I bussed tables at a sandwich shop. Looking back, busboy is probably the most profitable job anyone with a Com degree could hope for.

"Let's go to Papagayo's," Ryan said one night, sitting in the good camping chair—the one with a cupholder.

This seemed like a solid new way to meet people. Who better to befriend us than fellow drunks? *Drinkers were our people.* This couldn't fail!

"Okay," I said and we crossed Swan Road, past the Safeway,

to the strip mall housing a Mexican restaurant and cantina called Papagayo's.

The smell of chimichanga grease was airborne. The bar area was dark and crowded, which made it hard to introduce ourselves and chat. Even worse, it was karaoke night. Ryan and I were not singers, but were desperate for camaraderie. Anything was possible.

Anything, except actually making friends.

We ordered a pitcher of margaritas and sat down. In about five minutes, we realized there was a third population in Tucson beyond retirees and college coeds: divorcees. Papagayo's was a middle-aged pickup bar. The room was filled with men and women with suntan lines where wedding rings used to be.

We were 22 and intimidated by dudes who could afford to wash their clothes more than once a month. So, instead of saying "hi," we drank.

The more we drank, the bolder we grew about karaoke. A game developed where one person would secretly sign the other up for a song. We'd be desperately looking for kinship and hear the K-jay said, "Can I have *Ryan* up on stage. Ryan's going to sing 'These Boots Were Made for Walking.'"

"You bastard," he said, and went up on stage.

We drank several more margaritas, sizing up the crowd for anyone with something in common with us. Instead, we heard talk about soccer camps and stock options and careers not involving four-sided bagels.

Worse yet, our margaritas cost the entirety of both our bank accounts. We didn't realize this until looking at a menu. This would be a problem.

"Okay, I've got it," I told Ryan. "I'll just get kicked out."

"Sure, dude."

"We get kicked out. Then we won't have to pay!"

"How?"

"You signed me up to sing, right?"

"No."

"Dude."

"No."

"I'm serious."

"Forever in Blue Jeans," he mumbled.

25

"Watch this." I waited for my name to be called. Our margaritas were gone and my courage was high. I could've used it to talk and make friends, but instead I planned to alienate the entire room.

I planned to make people so uncomfortable they would yank the plug on the karaoke machine and throw me into the parking lot, barking about never being welcomed back.

In other words: *Free Margaritas!*

That math I could do.

My weapon of choice would not be feel-good Neil Diamond lyrics scrolling across the screen, but something with a little more firepower. The Butthole Surfers.

In a room full of accountants and housewives the Butthole Surfers couldn't fail.

I hopped up, grabbed the mic and barely waited for the synth notes to play. There are many offensive songs in the Butthole Surfers' catalog. In spite of the tequila in my system, I thought quick and chose to get tossed from Papagayo's with help from "The Shah Sleeps in Lee Harvey's Grave."

As Diamond's singalong hit played, I sang out of time and in a key of my own invention.

The tune, for those not familiar, is filled with rhyming non sequiturs describing the odd results of the singer's last trip to the restroom and the improbability of getting high from smoking Elvis' toenails. It was going to be a winner.

I sang with shoulders cringed, ready to be whisked through the door and dropped on my skull. I couldn't wait, really.

Let me reiterate: *Free Margaritas!*

I was a mathematical genius.

"Forever in Blue Jeans" ended but nothing happened. I was still on stage. Still lonely. Still broke.

"Let's hear it for Pat, ladies and gentleman," the jockey said.

And then…people sorta clapped.

"Well now," the bearded karaoke jock said. "That wasn't my cup of tea, but it was sure interesting. Good job!"

Cup of tea?

Good job?

Love and applause are great. Hatred is thrilling, too. But indifference is pure agony. Indifference is the worst salt any wound can welcome. It's the margarita rock salt of crowd reactions.

Clearly, Papagayo's patrons were actually pretty open minded. They probably would have made great friends. But at that point we were too poor and too embarrassed to stick around.

Defeated as karaoke outlaws, Ryan and I split the tab and exited penniless. He managed, as some sort of retribution, to steal one of the massive glass pitchers under his shirt. We were quiet walking back across Swan Road late at night with traffic dead, thinking about our latest friend-finding failure.

Being grown-up and alone was miserable. But, hey, it was my turn to sleep on the real mattress.

I smiled.

"Durango time, buddy," I told the only friend I had in the world.

DWIGHT STUFF

I've known Dwight Yoakam for many years. Almost a decade. Not in a personal, cracking open a few Budweisers in our lawn chairs, way. I honestly can't picture his face. Well, I can, but then something inside me says, "No wait, that's Alan Jackson," and then it counter-corrects and says, a little shaky: "Um, wait, maybe you're thinking of Michael Madsen in *Kill Bill*. He wore a cowboy hat, right?" And no, I don't really even know the man through his music.

I am probably the only man on Earth who knows Dwight Yoakam strictly through his food. And now I am in mourning.

My girlfriend, Leah, and I were more or less nomadic for a few years in the early 2000s. Ohio, Florida, Arizona and finally Oregon were places we called home. We were making a huge move from Tucson to Portland and realized there ain't a whole lot of anything between Las Vegas and San Francisco. Desert. Rocks. Highway. The World's Largest Thermometer. But then we hit California's famed San Joaquin Valley and the scenery turned to long green fields of lettuce and tomatoes and gigantic sprinkler systems. The World's Largest Salad, in essence.

Soundly in the center of this lushness is Bakersfield, where we spent a night. But what does one do for fun in Bakersfield? Why mosey down to Buck Owens' Crystal Palace, of course. Owens, the California country music king, was a lifelong Bakersfield resident and supposedly invented something called the "Bakersfield Sound," which by my best guess is country played to the rhythm of a lettuce sprinkler. The Crystal Palace wasn't too big on crystal and not much of a palace. Sort of a really ornamental Outback Steakhouse...but with a stage! I don't remember who performed that evening. They sang a song about the Martha White Flour Company, because the company was sponsoring this tour. This was my first exposure to the tangled bromance between music and food.

My next exposure came quickly—my entrée. I'm a sucker for menu items named for celebrities. So it was impossible not to order the Dwight Yoakam Baby Back Ribs. Like the flour-power band on stage, I can't remember anything about the food. But whenever I meet someone from Bakersfield, my reply is always: "Wonderful town. I stayed in Bakersfield once. Had the Dwight Yoakam ribs." And the general consensus of Bakersfieldians is that of confusion and, "what are you talking about?"

So imagine the confusion and "what are you talking about?" look I gave the freezer section of Walgreen's a few years later when I spotted Dwight Yoakam's line of frozen foods. Somehow this country star had graduated from having racks of ribs named in his honor to filling a freezer rack with an entire line of microwave food seemingly designed for stoned teenagers. Boxes featured Yoakam's silhouette and the I-only-did-this-for-the-cash slogan: "Just heat 'em and eat 'em."

My first sighting was the Chickin' Licken's Chicken Rings. "Odd," I thought. "What business does a country musician have deep frying chicken into circles? For that matter, what business does anyone have?" This food was a hilarious oddity that I couldn't help but walk by each time we visited the drugstore. I honestly looked forward to it, if for no other reason than the cheap smile the box provided.

Yoakam's line seemed to double every so often. Following the traditional rings, Chef Yoakam entered his Progressive period with the equally perplexing Rings of Fire (I bet Johnny Cash was pissed he didn't think of that first), quickly followed by Dwight Yoakam's Chicken Fries. "Seriously, Dwight," I thought as the years passed and Mr. Yoakam found increasingly creative ways to morph frozen chicken. "I'm a little embarrassed for you and I don't even know anything about you. Do you think Mrs. Butterworth or Betty Crocker would put their likeness on this stuff? Maybe that Gordon's Fisherman guy, but, come on, sailors will eat anything." Still, I smiled and chuckled and always visited the freezer section.

Next, Yoakam entered his Avant Garde period of microwave meal art. First, it was the Lickin' Chickin' Pizza Fries, which, I guess were breaded shards of chicken-pizza. But his Salvador Dali moment came courtesy of Dwight Yoakam's Macaroni Mouth Poppers. Yes, batter dipped, deep fried mac and cheese. At this point, my smiles and chuckles were transformed to stunned gawks.

This was getting out of hand. I began anticipating new Yoakam material the way his fans did his albums. What would Dwight, in some top secret Bakersfield test kitchen, invent next?

Sadly—like the last track of Dwight's famous album, *This Time*— his crowning achievement was followed by silence. A recent trip to Walgreen's revealed an empty slot in the freezer for all Yoakam's goodies and an empty slot in my heart. A quick look online showed all links for Yoakam's food company, Bakersfield Biscuits, to be dead.

This sucked the wind out of me. I felt responsible for Yoakam's failure. While I was always amused by his gastronomic stunts, I never once bought any. Maybe if I had, Dwight could've netted the capital to fund his secret culinary lab in the San Joaquin Valley. My point-and-laugh routine may have cost the world its only shot at Chicken Squares, Chicken Triangles, Chicken Rhomboids and maybe even Dwight Yoakam Baby Back Rib Tots.

Who else had the balls to push microwave cuisine that far?

Rest in peace.

This got me thinking about misguided celebrity foods. My eyes have always had a sixth-sense for famous faces at the grocery store. I'm not talking about Paul Newman's ridiculous line of Newman's Own Frozen Kimchi or Newman's Talcum Powder or whatever. I was never led to believe they were using Paul's personal recipe for knockoff Oreos. But Dwight was different. Chef Yoakam, I assumed, was the mastermind.

Dwight's rise to stoner cooking guru and decline back down to humble-everyday-average-country-singin'-millionaire mimicked that of Smokey Robinson's. Equally missing from grocery store shelves and the internet is Robinson's disturbingly rubberized face.

[**Wentastic Fact:** I originally thought this was poor graphic design, but I saw Robinson in person once and it looks like Mr. Motown was trying to fill up a *Buy 10 Facelifts Get 1 Free* card.] Smokey, a Detroit native, released his own line of frozen treats: Soul is in the Bowl Red Beans and Rice, Gumbo, and Pot Roast. Equally perplexing, equally embarrassing and I equally couldn't stop squealing in delight whenever I spotted one covered in freezer section fog.

It's no shock these products were born with one culinary foot in the grave. But why were they there in the first place? Should we blame musicians struggling with hefty facelift debts? Money-hungry microwave food corporations? Niche fans who purchase food a favorite singer supposedly created?

No. The man to blame is Jimmy Dean…and to a lesser degree, Kenny Rogers.

Not to be confused with movie star James Dean, Jimmy was a country singer in the 50s and 60s, peaking with the still-awesome tune, "Big Bad John." Jimmy actually tried a movie career, costarring in James Bond's *Diamonds are Forever*, but like Yoakam and Robinson after him, found his true home in the grocer's freezer.

In 1969 Jimmy began selling sausage. Who knows why? Desperate men do desperate things during desperate times. Maybe this was his last resort against economic ruin? Regardless, Jimmy Dean Sausages featured his picture on every tube of fatty breakfast fun and included the singer in commercials. These foods are, to my knowledge, still around.

Seeing this success from his mountaintop fortress, Kenny Rogers stoked his snowy beard and declared he, too, would like to be a singer and food entrepreneur. This, of course, led to the foundation of Kenny Rogers Roasters. Made ultra-famous in a Seinfeld skit where Kramer was tortured and infatuated by the rotisserie birds, the restaurant was apparently handcuffed to Boston Market as they both fell down the mine shaft of poultry obscurity. [**WENTASTIC FACT:** There are still 37 Kenny Rogers restaurants in business, all, oddly, located in the Philippines.]

Following *Seinfeld*, I guess singers took a hint that there may be quick money to be made in chow.

After all this research and reminiscing, I left a trail of macaroni poppers, gumbo and chicken bones in my wake, but no answers. What makes a man—this phenomenon seems to be focused pretty heavily on dudes, though Madonna did apparently try to shill her own wine for a while—decide to sell his soul to sell his bowls? I'm no marketing exec, but Billboard Chart success does not instantly translate into microwave meal millions. It's not like Emeril Legasse is cutting country records or Colonel Sanders ever released a hiphop mix tape [**Wentastic Fact:** Though, Corbin, KY's favorite son did once release a Christmas album].

Today, I'm sitting at my desk, thinking deeply on the subject of chicken rings and country music sausage and you know what? I don't care what makes these crooners run to the kitchen. I'm just sad to see them disappear. Dwight and Smokey, they took a swing at frozen food for some odd reason and I support it. It's what makes waking up worth it some days. Not that they are actually producing food, which is pretty damn irrelevant at this point, but that there are still surprises in this life.

Information whips through our consciousness so quickly and easily now. It's the little *found* surprises that make me happiest. So bring it on. I might not buy this stuff, but if I ever see Travis Tritt's Shrimp 'n' Grits, it'll make me grin and that's worth a little failure.

SIEGFRIED, PASS ME A DRUMSTICK

Rumor has it, Keith Moon, the drummer for The Who, swallowed so many horse tranquilizers he fell off the drum set during the first song of a concert. They couldn't get him to blink, let alone play "My Generation." The band announced to the crowd: *if anyone thinks they can handle playing with us, give it a shot.* Turned out, one guy in the audience was a huge Moon fan. So huge he'd learned the beats to every tune. That guy got to rock out with The Who for one night and became an urban legend.

My story isn't so exciting. But then again, that one didn't involve magic spells from Siegfried and Roy.

I spent the weekend in Las Vegas for my bachelor party. Sunday night we eat dinner at the Haufbrau House, a German beer hall-style restaurant. It's a massive Bavarian barn with long picnic tables, waitresses who carry beer steins and dress in traditional *Heidi*-type yodeling dresses. Also there is a live polka band with a shitcan-drunk drummer who makes everyone toast at least once every 10 minutes.

Beer is served in mugs the size of small gas tanks. Pretty much everything on the menu involves sausage. There is even a sexy woman going table to table selling fresh pretzels.

So the oompa music is stomping and we're drinking until our eyes start to cross when the lovely young singer in the band taps me on the shoulder and tells me to come with her.

If you and I were sitting down, sharing ice cream, you might ask me at this point: "How did she know it was your bachelor party?"

Then I'd reply, "Oh, yeah. I forgot to mention the hat."

Since it is my bachelor party, Medved, Ben and Don decide to inflict maximum torture by forcing me to wear a three-foot tall dunce cap. It is pretty obvious something is going on. Our waitress had asked earlier about the cap. She, I assume, parlayed the info to the band.

I stagger up on stage and the entire group kicks into a tuba-filled version of some number that roughly means, "We Lift You up with Our Song." Two hundred people stare at some drunk in a dunce cap.

The band finishes and, relieved that is the end, I hop offstage.

"No, no, no," the drunk drummer says. "It is traditional for the bachelor to play an instrument. Here, you play my drums?" he says with a slurred German accent.

"Um, Okay."

"Here," he says, tugging at his shoulder strap. "You wear my lederhosen?"

It's pretty clear I don't want to find out what's under his short-shorts, so I decline. In retrospect, I wish I hadn't. How much better would this story be if I was wearing lederhosen?

There are no horse tranquilizers involved, but this is starting to look like the Who-thing.

I sit down and I'm guessing 99% of the people expect a disaster. But I have a secret. Since we moved from Tucson to Portland, Leah joined a band. My fiancée taught me how to play the drums and I can stumble through a few beats.

The accordion and the tuba start up and the female singer lays into something German and I give 'em the old *Boom-Thwack-Boom*.

Needless to say, some drunk kid in a dunce cap, beating the drums with a polka band gets people clapping and yelling. I am some slow-witted German kid brother of Keith Moon for a couple minutes.

The tune ends and I feel pretty good that this is the craziest thing that'll happen to me for a long time.

The drummer wanders back up all google-eyed: "You drink beer?"

"I love beer."

"Good. Bring it up on stage."

I scurry back and get my mammoth mug, which is a little under half full. I estimate that's still about two regular beers. And I'm told I have five seconds to drink it all.

The drummer stands on his stool and beats on the drums, counting.

"ONE!"

I chug.

"TWO!"

I nearly vomit.

"THREE."

I chug.

"FOUR!"

I finish.

"FIVE!"

People go nuts.

I nearly vomit.

This is now officially the coolest dinner of my life.

I nearly vomit.

I rejoin the table and we order approximately 10 gallons worth of beer.

By pals consider desert and drink more beer and the band kicks out some more songs. At one point they bust out a giant Ricola commercial horn that takes two people to carry. They parade it around the room tooting a mountain song or something.

Things are pretty awesome at this point, but still not as awesome as the guy with The Who.

Until things get interesting.

Commercials make us believe that Vegas is this crazy city where people win a ton of money and make love to strippers every night. Supposedly, Wayne Newton stops by your room to see if you'd like to grab a martini. But most people who've been there know you leave poor, the town is dirty and crowded, and there are people giving out hookers' business cards every seven feet. Most gamblers wear sweatpants.

But imaginary Vegas waves its magic wand over the Haufbrau House tonight.

The band stops playing and patrons start standing and clapping. We turn around and there's a man in a wheelchair.

"Oh, shit, that's Roy," Ben, says.

Sure enough. One half of the white tiger-loving magic team, Siegfried and Roy, is here.

"You know," our waiter says. "Siegfried is here, too."

I nearly vomit.

Shining like the million dollars of plastic surgery he is, Siegfried walks in, waves and poses for a quick photo with the band.

We get up so I can bum rush him and get a picture taken, too.

Here's something you might not know about a man who earns a living making tigers disappear: He is exceptionally quick and agile. Especially when half-drunk bachelors in dunce caps begin stalking him.

I am close enough to smell the tiger sweat on his neck. But something stops me from grabbing Siggy's shoulder and asking to pose for a snapshot.

Somehow, in my drunken buzz, I regain what doctors call: "common sense."

Suddenly, I don't want to force this man to take a shot with me. Suddenly, I don't want to get in his way as he simply tries to find the door.

This doesn't sound like me.

In retrospect, all I can think of is that he used some sort of White Tiger ESP on me. The same brain magic he uses when he wants a 2,000 pound cat to magically pull a bouquet of roses out of his pants pocket.

So, no, the house polka band isn't exactly The Who. So maybe I won't go down in urban legend history. But that guy in the 70s didn't have a magic spell cast on him by a homosexual magician, did he?

VOODOO WEDDING

Okay, let's pretend for a few minutes that you are my son or daughter. It's a stretch to assume I'm not shooting blanks, but just play along. As a Wensink, you will eventually get curious about mom and dad. Someday in the distant future, you will care enough to ask about my most romantic day.

I'll kick this fairytale off with something like: Well, it all starts when a jittery minister in a tuxedo jacket feeds me a doughnut. Your mother is in a long white gown on the other side licking frosting off her lips. It stinks like fried dough and sugary jelly filling. It's the smell of love.

Two minutes earlier: I say a prayer to a velvet painting of Issac Hayes with 30 friends. We are clown-car tight. It reminds me of throwing a dance party in my freshman dorm. The room isn't much bigger, but it smells better than Founder's Hall.

I take a bite from the "Cruller of Love" and sadly, the wedding is almost over.

Someday, my son or daughter, I'll tell you this exact tale. It'll probably be just as hazy, since I have a horrible memory.

It's the story of how your mother and I got hitched. That is, how we got married in a doughnut shop.

All ceremony long people are daring us to eat a pastry shaped like a penis and testicles.

Tonight it has "The Hedgehog" written in white icing across its shaft. This refers to the news that porn legend Ron Jeremy (whose nickname is Hedgehog, for reasons I don't want to know about) is in town this week. Tempting as a seven-inch edible phallus may be, we

37

have bigger business at hand.

Voodoo Doughnuts is quickly becoming the number one roadside attraction in town since we moved to Portland a few years ago. It's racing ahead of the white slavery tunnel tours. The velvet painting museum can't even see Voodoo's taillights. It's the kind of place that serves doughnuts topped with maple and bacon. The kind of place that fries up bear claws with grape Kool-Aid and Froot Loops in the frosting. The kind of place the FDA once shut down for injecting their pastries with Nyquil and Pepto Bismol.

It's the kind of doughnut shop that will legally marry you.

For $150 you and your mate's knot officially gets tied in the State of Oregon. The fee for wedded bliss also includes doughnuts and coffee for 10. Ask your local church if they can make a promise like that.

Both owners, Tres and Kat Daddy, are ordained ministers.

Tres is our man tonight. He's a pipe cleaner of an officiate who darts around as if he's just beer bonged espresso. But his service is surprisingly tender and sweet. It's as touching as one can get when you relate a marriage to the dips and peaks of a frosted cruller.

Before we share this symbolic doughnut, Tres packs all of our friends into the room. It's painted pastry-box pink and covered in tacky signs and a giant papier-mâché doughnut. The color is fitting, since it's hardly big enough for a baker's dozen inside. We're all jammed in, Leah and I with our backs to the bathroom. This is when we all look above us to the velvet shot of Isaac Hayes in all his bald beauty. After asking Black Moses' blessing, we're encouraged to stomp and scream in order to conjure up the voodoo spirits.

Following the ceremonial cruller, Tres talks us into delivering our own vows while he, "Writes voodoo stuff on the floor." Leah and I stumble through some unrehearsed words about how hot one another is, while Tres scrambles around scratching out hieroglyphics that only make sense if one's brain is 90% espresso.

Next, he passes a bucket of Froot Loops around the audience. He waits a few seconds, then pronounces us man and wife. At this point 30 people bomb us with loose breakfast cereal.

We crunch our way out the door, officially man and wife in the eyes of the doughnut gods.

THE CURSE OF THREES

"Any day of the week, mother fucker!"

Put yourself in my shoes. It's midnight on a Friday a few weeks ago. You and your wife are walking out of a bar called Holocene back toward your bicycles. It's not the best part of Portland. But then again, it's not the worst. At least you thought so about four seconds ago.

You are still discussing how your wife nearly got into a fight at the bar—stone sober no less—when you hear a man's squirrelly voice come from the convenience store parking lot to your left.

"Any day of the week, mother fucker!"

Here's a list of things that the other half of this conversation may have said before you walked past:

1. "Thanks so much for helping my boyfriend and I move. We'd like to have you over for dinner, when's a good time for you?"

2. "Math really isn't my best subject. Can we sit down for a study group before finals?"

3. "Hi there, my name's Karl Motherfucker. I'm new in town. Could you tell me when the mall is open here in Portland?"

Sadly, your hopes are stomped when you realize this voice belongs to a guy pointing a dull black handgun into the driver's side of a parked car. Clearly, nobody's going to be reading over their calculus books any time soon. What you don't realize is that you are waist deep in the **curse of threes**.

I've never been overly superstitious. I don't worry about broken mirrors or walking under ladders. I'm pretty confident Michael Keaton isn't showing up if I say, "*Beetlejuice,*" three times.

The one that's always stuck with me, however, is that bad things happen in threes. I don't know where this legend started, but it seems to crop up in my life on a semi-regular basis. If I stub my toe, chances are I'll jam a finger and poke out my eye.

The worst part is that you really don't realize you're on a bad luck skid until after the third thing happens and you can look back on this misfortune. Such was the case that night.

Get back into my shoes: You start off well by meeting friends and catching up at Holocene. The bar is super crowded, the kind of crowded where you have to wedge yourself in line with a pick-ax and a flashlight. While packed into this logjam your wife commits the unforgivable sin of stepping in front of a drunk girl.

"Uhhhh, *excuse* me, bitch," she mutters in the classic "I'm pretending to say this to my date, but in reality I'm saying it loudly enough for everyone to hear," fashion. "We're *all* going to get drinks. No need to cut."

This is the part where you and your wife try to explain that, in fact, we're just closing our tab. Actually, you tell the drunk girl, I have the credit card, so my wife isn't really a problem.

This is where her not-so-private conversation about how big of a bitch you married continues.

Now you offer to let her in front of both of you to get her drink, to which she replies, "Oh no, I'm fine...it's cool." And turns around and complains at the top of her lungs.

Well, people start to yell and drunk girls get huffy, but the good news is, nobody got in a fight. But it was touch-and-go for a while there.

Which brings you back to: "Any day of the week, mother fucker!"

In a perfect world you'd disarm this gunman with a shoe and make the cover of the Sunday paper. But in a perfect world you wouldn't be walking past a convenience store full of gun nuts. So you take your chances and run across four lanes of traffic to the other side of the road.

Luckily, there are no shots fired as you scurry down the sidewalk. Unfortunately, you are only two-thirds done with your unlucky streak.

Here is where you two find your bikes around the corner, stripped of their head and tail lights.

Well now it all hits you. Not just your wife complaining about how she told you not to park our bikes here—which she did. You've just been sideswiped by the old unlucky skid. **The curse of threes**.

But wait.

Things could have been worse. You could have had your teeth punched out by a drunk girl's boyfriend. You could have caught a bullet in the thigh. Your entire bicycle could have been stolen.

Maybe bad things don't happen in threes. Just things that could have been worse. It's not exactly optimism, but you'll take it. Some sunshine in your outlook is always needed. Hey, you just landed your first fulltime job with benefits and all (after three years of temps and unemployment). Cheer up.

So now, if anyone wants to join me, I'm going to walk under a ladder, looking into a broken mirror, saying "Beetlejuice," three times. Luck is on our side.

When?

"Any day of the week, mother fucker!"

HOW I LEARNED TO STOP WORRYING
AND LOVE MELLENCAMP

It's hot today, but it doesn't feel like summer until I listen to Seymour, Indiana's favorite son. It wasn't always this easy. It took a lot of growing up to release my inner-Hoosier.

Here's how:

There was a lull in the conversation on our way to the grocery store. I decided it was time to open up, to make my feelings public and impossible to take back. It was a moment that arrives in every marriage, I assumed. A difficult moment of raw honesty.

"Honey, I think I'm a John Mellencamp kinda guy."

This was the step alcoholics take at their first group meetings. That day, the road to recovery was paved with copies of "Pink Houses."

My wife sat silent for a second. "Oh, okay," she said.

As we pulled into the store, it became painfully obvious she didn't appreciate this breakthrough. She didn't comprehend how massive this moment was.

Why would she? She's a girl.

At age 26, I finally put a longstanding prejudice to rest. I embraced the Coug' so much, he became my summer soundtrack.

But from age 14-26 I hated John for one reason: Girls.

According to my research, Mellencamp is one of only three Indianans of note. The others being Michael Jackson and Larry Bird. That's pretty good. I grew up one state east and Ohio's top pop culture contribution was America's fattest president.

Sure, Hoosier-state jealousy played a role in this Mellencamp rage, but not completely. The problem was all Midwestern girls, age

14-26, loved John Cougar Mellencamp. There was once an obscure law stating girls had to sing "Jack and Diane" at the top of their lungs if the temperature rose above 75-degrees and two-to-eight girls were in the car. Needless to say, this was annoying for 14-to-26-year-old boys. There was a serious lack of understanding between the two demographics since the only music boys sang together usually involved Lars Ulrich and James Hetfield.

But really, there is no problem with any sex singing any song at the top of their lungs. The real sand in my shoes was simple: I was convinced Midwestern girls, ages 14-26, had terrible taste in music.

A sample CD collection of any girl my age from Cleveland to Kansas City at the time featured hearty doses of The Eagles *Greatest Hits*, U2 *Greatest Hits*, Natalie Merchant *Tigerlilly*, probably one, if not two, Shania Twain records, Tom Petty *Greatest Hits*, Bryan Adams *Greatest Hits*, Madonna *Immaculate Collection* and of course…John Cougar Mellencamp *Greatest Hits*.

In my teens, being an enlightened (also known as "Snobby") Midwestern music fan whose pride and joy was a complete Sonic Youth discography, I deduced any artist owned by a 14-to-26-year-old female must suck.

This wasn't just my theory. My friends, 14-to-26-year-old Midwestern boys (also known as Metallica fans), made sure anyone caught humming melodies from the above albums would be publicly humiliated in ways 14-to-26-year-old Midwestern boys specialize in. This was double-true for anyone spotted within five yards of a Natalie Merchant record.

Frankly, I'm okay with that rule still applying.

So, how did I come to this heavenly-beam-of-light realization that I was a Mellencamp kinda guy?

Beats me.

Chances are, it revolved around the fact that I wasn't 16 anymore. Things that I thought sucked back then (**see also**: vegetables, John Cougar Mellencamp, my parents) were quite enjoyable. It just took time and maturity to appreciate these gifts. Once I'd grown into a husband and broader music connoisseur (still known as "Snobby"), I fully appreciated ditties like "Lonely Ol' Night."

Suddenly, summer wasn't summer without The Coug'. Once my heart opened and my stereo filled with farmland anthems, I learned

JCM and I have a lot in common. For one: Indiana and Ohio are the heartland of America and are such close neighbors there's no way to know where one's cornfields begin and the other's end. Strip away each state's obese presidents and blonde mustached basketball stars and they're basically the same. Secondly, I was also born in a small town. Deshler, OH: population 1,831. And since I'm not a psychic, it is possible that I will die in a small town, much like the Mellencamp song. Finally, I also fought authority and authority also won. When I was 17, I was arrested in Deshler. As Professor Mellencamp can attest, small town police have too much time on their hands. Hence, the first notch was carved in my arrest record: *loitering*.

My wife and I got out of the car and I felt sort of embarrassed. Not for my secret fantasy of making love to "Human Wheels," but for the amount of time I dedicated to admitting I had a Mellencampiphany.

The 16-year-old Me would be surprised that, 10 years later, this is what I wasted my time on. Here I am, married and living in a new millennium filled with a dangerous recession, frightening violence, and free pornography. Meanwhile, I spend my time wondering about the existential implications of owning *Lonesome Jubilee*.

It is clear I am not the man I planned to become so many years ago.

I am not worried about the fact that our kids will be brought into a world where they have a 99% likelihood of becoming a meth addict. Past-tense Me would be pretty concerned about the amount of time adult Me has spent receiving food stamps and unemployment as he swims up this polluted river we call the job market. Although, 16-year-old me would be pretty psyched that a woman agreed to sleep with us on regular basis.

Me at 26 has come to grips that, yes, I am a Mellencamp man. He realizes that, yes, vegetables are delicious. He also sees that as you grow, you learn that stuff you once resisted is often exactly what you need.

But even if we never see eye-to-eye, at least young Me and now Me agree to tone down the Metallica and point and laugh at anyone listening to Natalie Merchant. Some things a man doesn't grow into. *Tigerlilly* tops that list.

PAT, THE PANTS AND THE PRISON

I'm standing in the same spot Bruce Willis and Billy Bob Thorton have, but I'm wearing another man's pants. There's a guy holding a rifle right above my head who claims he could kill me from a hundred yards away. I'm warned that any moment I could be held hostage by convicted felons and nobody is responsible for my well-being.

Welcome to the Oregon State Penitentiary (OSP), the Beaver State's only maximum-security jail.

Not many office field trips require a background check, but this is no normal outing. It also includes a metal detector sweep and, unknown to me, a strict dress code.

I show up to work ready to tour the biggest set of iron bars in Oregon, ready for a prison riot, ready for inmate catcalls…ready, possibly, to be stabbed with a knife carved from soap.

"Dude," my supervisor says first thing. "Didn't you get the email? What are you wearing?"

I am a bottom rung legal assistant with Portland's public defender. My office is really laid back. So relaxed, it's perfectly acceptable for your supervisor to call you, "dude." Luckily, it's also the kind of employer that offers educational visits to the state pen.

"What?" I say, dressed like I do every day: Sweater, jeans and tennis shoes. If I had slipped into a fish net tank-top and biker shorts I can see where I might get into a jam during our tour of the maximum security jail.

"The *jeans*," he says, expecting me to get it.

We kind of eye each other, waiting for someone to fill in the enormous gap here. Overhead fluorescent bulbs click in the silence.

"You can't wear jeans to a prison," he says.

"You can't?"

"The inmates wear jeans. You might get mistaken for a prisoner," he tells me in a *duh* kind-of-voice. "Didn't you get the email?"

Obviously not. Luckily, my work provides dress clothes to clients who can't afford them. We have a fully stocked walk-in closet.

I borrow a pair of brown slacks and a recent memo from another co-worker whispers into my ear. "*Wash your hands a lot. I just went to the doctor and was diagnosed with a staph infection on my legs. Even though my legs never touched a client, somehow their bedbugs decided to get into my skin.*"

Could these be the pants of the staph infection guy? Even though the office washes the clothes after they're worn, can you truly disinfect a staph infection? Should I try another pair? What if *those* are the infected pants? What if they have something worse, like hepatitis? Maybe I'm lucky with a staph infection.

My legs start itching immediately.

The big house, while scarved in barbed wire and a huge concrete wall, doesn't quite look like movies and TV and video games want you to think prison does.

The walls are canary yellow. Not brick red. Not granite gray. It may as well be molded from Easter Peeps. I'm sure some board of directors sat down and digested a lot of research to find out what color best expresses, "Cheer up, you're only doing twenty-to-life."

The entire place is some skull-crushing mix of pop culture myth and dark reality. Fact and fiction play the old switcharoo, wearing one-another's pants like a bizarre prison escape plan.

"Welcome to OSP, I have to warn you, there is always a risk of being wounded, taken hostage..." our tour guide, Aaron, says. He's a beefy fella with a mustache. He could juggle three of me he's so big. Aaron warns us of other horrible, Chuck Norris-type scenarios that can happen. But I am zoned out from fear. I snap back when he says: "We *do not* negotiate with hostage takers. Even if the Governor himself were taken in, we'd treat him the same as you."

I find this hard to believe. I check over my shoulder, Oregon

Governor Ted Kolungoski is nowhere to be seen. Now I'm worried

After checking us for guns and knives made of soap the guards lock our small group behind iron bars. This is where Aaron drops the next payload. "We have about twenty-two hundred inmates here. However, we only have about thirty-five guards on duty."

I'm not making it out alive. Thanks to budget cutbacks this place is teetering on the edge of a prison riot and I'm a pasty chunk of meat for inmates to pass around. The only thing keeping me from huddling into a sobbing-wet ball on the floor is the security of knowing murderers, rapists, drug addicts and art forgers are locked up tight, surviving on bread and water as I walk around catching unknown diseases from itchy pants.

This, like what color prison walls are, is a myth that pop culture has pulled over my eyes.

We walk through another huge, bright yellow steel door into the artery of this monster. There is a riot on the horizon.

Hundreds of prisoners swarm in and out of doors—unaccompanied by guards—free to stab and strangle and forge Picassos at will. But they mostly just stare and scurry along like they're late to algebra.

None of the guards seem to mind, so I assume this is normal. And sure enough, everyone wears denim: jeans, jean jackets, even jean shirts. It's like a John Denver clothing catalogue, but with lots of tattoos.

Cell Block C is first on our tour. To my surprise, it actually *looks* like a prison. Five stories of shoebox cells and thick bars. It's long and holds about a quarter of the inmates. It'd be really depressing too, if every cell wasn't painted a different shade of cutesy pastel.

The colors gently remind prisoners: "Look on the bright side, Inmate #76990, at least you're not in The Hole."

Cells are cramped and dark and the inmates are respectfully quiet. Nobody tosses buckets of urine at us. Nobody blows the harmonica. Catcalls are nil.

We exit back into a sandpit of denim and glares. Our guide ushers our group to the corner and explains that outdoor time in the Yard is over and inmates are heading back to their cells. Everyone, without exception, stares.

What did that guy do? I wonder. Armed robbery? Kidnapping? Molesting grown men in borrowed corduroy pants?

"I would estimate," Aaron says, unprovoked. "That eighty-percent of the men you see right now are sex offenders."

Even my staph infection gets the heebie-jeebies.

I've never been undressed with someone's eyes, but I assume inmates are stripping me right now. I get the sudden urge to apologize to every model ever seen in one of my sister's *Cosmo* magazines when I was a kid.

Before this morning, I assumed the Yard was nothing more than a weight bench and a mud pit. This too, is a myth. The Yard is huge, offering five basketball courts, sand volleyball, miniature golf course, a garden, a running track, telephones and even two softball fields

Apparently, OSP hosts summer tournaments with local softball teams of citizens. Something tells me stealing third is natural to the OSP Fighting Eagles.

What other myths were debunked on my trip?

Prison food consists of bread, water and loaves of cooked entrails: Lunch today is chicken parmesan and pulled pork for dinner. The cafeteria looks a lot like my high school one, except the prisoners have a Coke fountain. What does that say about public schools?

Inmates sit around all day planning new ways to carve knives out of soap: Wrong again. Almost all prisoners are required to work at one of the three onsite factories—the state's third largest laundry facility, a metal shop and a furniture shop. Once, Aaron says, an inmate actually sewed himself into a couch to escape. He didn't get far.

Surprisingly, all the furniture is made for government offices and state colleges (like the prisoner-invented "Indestructible Dorm Chairs").

I take comfort knowing while Governor Kolungoski isn't here to bail me out of a riot, he is probably typing at a desk made by an inmate.

There is a magic button, just like in the movies, that opens all the cell doors and frees the prisoners to riot and murder: Still wrong. I specifically ask Aaron and he assures me that would be the worst addition any prison could make. But they do have switches that *close* all the doors and other switches to cut the power or the water and utilities in case of riots.

Wonderful, I think. So while some art forger holds me hostage with a soap knife to my throat I won't even be able to flush the toilet.

People get tossed in "The Hole": If there's really a Hole, they hide it well. OSP has certain levels of security for rambunctious dudes, but even death row inmates are given 45 minutes of outdoor time a day.

Next we stand alongside a huge razor wire fence circling the Yard. Aaron asks if anyone's ever seen the film, *Bandits*. This is the spot where Bruce Willis and Billy Bob Thorton escape from prison in a cement truck.

The Hollywood crew actually set up shop and filmed here because unlike most maximum security Hiltons, OSP still has a mean-ass concrete wall that people imagine when they think of prison, albeit the same color as a rubber ducky.

Luckily, Aaron and his mustache aren't just shattering myths today. Here are some truths about prison, as well.

It smells bad. Oddly, the entire place, especially the high security area, smells like onions.

Tower guards shoot to kill. As far as I can tell, yes. Like I said, guards are trained to hit someone a football field away. And to prove they mean business there are strategic pits of sand around the perimeter. This allows sharpshooters to pop off a warning bullet into something other than my stomach. Eerily enough, each one has a smiley face etched into it.

It's pretty freaking impossible to escape. The old "dig a tunnel" routine won't work unless that inmate is part sea lion. OSP purposely dropped its cheerful yellow wall 10 feet into the ground, which is about where the water shelf begins. So in order to get under the wall, you also have to go underwater.

You're also not going to hop in a laundry sack and get smuggled out with the dirty underwear. OSP figured this one out by using some super-monitor at the gates that detects motion. According to the guide, this machine is so sensitive it can tell if a cat's heart is thumping in the truck. My tax dollars hard at work.

But as anyone who's ever been stabbed by a soapy knife can tell you, prisoners are always thinking of new ways to beat the system. Watch out, Aaron.

Next is the maximum security bunker. It's three stories of Oregon's worst criminals and our guide eagerly shows us around. Inside, it's a state-of-the-art chimpanzee cage. This place is dark and circular and heavily guarded. The cells are bare with Plexiglas covering the bars. Nothing is painted to resemble an Easter egg. This room would split Hannibal Lecter in two.

Finally, the biggest myth debunked is at the opposite end of this building where men are executed.

The death chamber is a dungeon with iron shackles and water dripping from the ceiling. It looks, oddly, like my cubicle at work. Except *it* has a window…though to the viewing room.

There's a flimsy partition where executioner sits and on the other side is a hospital bed with lots of leather straps. According to our guide, they inject the condemned with enough poison to murder a horse.

I'm standing close enough to smell the clean white linens on the stretcher. Once again, my scabies get the scabies and I exit.

On my way out, one final myth is verified.

The governor can stop an execution. Next to the exit is a little red phone labeled, "Governor". It leads to a little red phone on Kolungoski's OSP-prisoner-made desk. I think about picking it up and asking if he knows what happens if he's caught in the middle of a prison. But I assume I'll earn a pastel cell of my own.

Just like everything else in this world portrayed by television and movies, prison is a mixture of fact and fiction and the truth is a lot less romantic than we'd like to think. But it's not the end of the world. Remember what the yellow cell tells us, "Life without parole ain't so bad, at least you don't have a soap knife in your back."

UNCOMFORTABLY NUMB

You just paid six bucks to stare at the biggest set of balls in history. Exotic, Swedish testicles. But this wasn't part of the deal. At least you didn't think so. It's at this very moment, watching a pair of sweaty Nordic cherries on the big screen, that it hits you: Nothing's really shocking anymore.

Portland's third annual Grindhouse Film Fest promised to be a weekend spotlighting history's squishiest, bloodiest, stomach-flipping-est flicks. The festival's website promised gore, revenge and, yes, sex. But this? Nowhere in the two newspaper articles you read was there any mention of the sweatiest of the sweaty.

Not that the crowd wasn't ready for balls. Frankly, the mob of hundreds thought it was great, what with all the squeals and cheers.

See, you and your buddy from work, Tim, are lured into the final film of this three day puke-fest, an obscure 1973 Swedish picture, *They Call Her One-Eye*. A picture reportedly combining an eye patch-wearing teenage girl, buckets of blood, sex slavery, kung-fu, guns, revenge, a SEXY one-eyed SWEDISH teenage girl, and—the knockout punch: the promise of this being, "the most obscene film in history."

Now, if there's one thing the internet has taught you, it's that there's a lot of obscene footage out there. Right now you're ranking about a dozen different filthy online moments involving anything from barn animals to plastic vampire teeth. So when something claims to be the tops in this crowded field, it gets your attention.

Problem is, every day you have an information seizure. The world is so focused on myth-busting that the exotic idea of a film turning

51

your face green becomes intriguing. There really are no mysteries left. The Loch Ness Monster was all plywood, Houdini was just a good actor, Dolly Parton's boobs are made by Goodyear.

So, a flick about a Swedish teen prostitute with a chip on her shoulder makes you feel like Neil Armstrong. You're boldly going where no man has before. You're staring at the unknown, waiting to see who blinks first.

Sadly, the unknown looks like an enormous pink nutsack.

Like Nessie, Houdini and Dolly, the mystery surrounding sexy eye-patched Swedes is a better idea than the actual flickering product. In the myth department, the film scores an A+. From the moment you promised the ticket taker, "I will not ask for my money back, no matter how offended I get," until the movie started, your anxiety was working third shift.

"What can possibly be so offensive?" you and Tim wonder while the crowd shuffles in. "What kind of cruel, blood-smeared revenge do these Viking bastards have in store?"

Mostly, you worry this is a bad idea. "Is this the kind of thing that'll warp my mind? I've heard everyone on earth is only a few steps away from being a serial killer. Is this the final straw on my camel's back?"

Tim doesn't seem as worried as you. He doesn't lose sleep regarding the moral implications of watching a movie. You kind of feel like Tipper Gore by comparison.

Regardless, it all comes back to, "What can be *this* offensive?" You are reminded of barn animals, plastic vampire teeth, German stuff.

In the end, the planet's most offensive film is just hype. You paid six dollars to see a poorly disguised porno on the big screen. A poorly disguised porno with a passion for ballsack close-ups. There is blood. There is revenge. There is one-eyed teenage prostitute kung-fu, but it's not as cool as it sounds. None of it is.

Maybe we are obsessed with debunking mysteries because we are scared not to? Have the economic lies and the war lies and the political poker faces of the last few years spoiled our love of surprise? Maybe we debunk because all our surprises are bad ones.

Like all mysteries in the 21st Century, *They Call Her One-Eye* is pure build-up. It's a great idea that is better in your imagination. You realize nothing will shock you more than the fear of the unknown.

Nothing makes the back of your neck sweat like being unaware of the darkness your brain can create.

Nothing, of course, except 20-foot Swedish testicles.

ANARCHIST CLOWNS STOLE MY MONEY

It's four in the afternoon on a weekday. The girl on the sidewalk, a few feet away, growls through a didgeridoo, taking occasional cigarette breaks. Across the street, punk rock circus clowns slap together a stage in their front yard. I'm just one of hundreds who skipped work or a strict bong regimen to unfold a card table in the hot sun. But I'm the only one with two gallons of barbecue sauce and a plan to get filthy rich.

This sidewalk doesn't get interesting until one of the clowns— sensibly dressed in only a leather jacket, jean shorts, cowboy boots and KISS makeup—rides a tricycle through the busy street. He's twanging a banjo, steering with his knees and nearly flattening himself in oncoming traffic. He's sort of the opening act—the warm-up comedian before Richard Pryor steps onstage.

How did I get here and how do I plan on making so much money?

Usually, people start a business by opening a little corner store or setting up a website. For some reason, I pitch my capitalistic career into action with a collapsible table at the intersection of Unsafe Clown Boulevard and Stupidity-with-Fire Avenue. Portland, OR's Last Thursday Street Fair is the only place in town *anybody* can sell *anything*. There are no rules or regulations or forms to sign. If you suspect it's the kind of place a guy with no food handler's license and even less culinary experience can hustle homemade barbecue sauce for six-bucks a jar, you'd be right.

It's not a flea market and it's not *really* a fair. Actually, it's some lawless gang-bang of art and garbage...and BBQ sauce. The girls on my left sell pencil sketches for $40 a frame (didgeridoo concerts are free, I guess). The ladies on the other side push hand-made necklaces and purses. Elsewhere, down about a mile's worth of Alberta Street, amateur businessmen hawk everything from welded Socrates sculptures to possibly-stolen tube socks at rock bottom prices. It's the last open market economy in America. The perfect salve for economic tough times we've been burned by. The only rule is: stay on the sidewalk. But that rule, apparently, doesn't apply to guerrilla clowns with impatient landlords.

My suspicions get hot when the Clown House (the tenement across the street hosting the face-painted madness) has its reggae band warm up at the volume of a Led Zepplin concert, followed shortly by an eating contest on the porch. (I'm reminded that my buddy, Ben, would mop the floor with these Barnum and Bailey rejects.)

At this point I realize capitalism is a brutal racket. Getting filthy wealthy is tougher than it looks. Contrary to my belief, Wentastic BBQ Sauce won't sell itself. Especially with this competition.

Ah, yes, Wentastic BBQ.

Don't you already know?

It's the jar with my picture on the label, cross-eyed drunk. No? Man, I should talk to the shareholders about this. Well, if there were a press release, it would read like this: "I've always had a special knack for public embarrassment. At the same time, I have a lust for food. My BBQ sauce stems from the natural desire to fuse both talents into a single, awkward, money-hungry machine. Thus, Wentastic Enterprises opened its *Barbecue Sauce Technologies* division."

It felt like success was already ringing my doorbell. What could be more of a no-brainer: Warm Weather + BBQ Grills + Food + Handsome Sidewalk BBQ Sauce Salesman = Early Retirement. A resignation letter to work was typed up and all but inked with my signature.

Turns out, when a thousand people shuffle by your little homemade BBQ sauce stand, only about every hundredth swings in for a free bite. Most passers-by are creeped out, even with a handsome sauce salesman. If taste testers weren't a big enough hurdle between me and a sack of cash, the brave free samplers were. They voiced concerns like: "Hey, there's no ingredient list here," "Ewww, how many people have touched these samples?" and, "Are you licensed to sell food to humans?" And most important, "Did you put drugs in this?"

Meanwhile, drug addicted anarchist clowns draw huge crowds and applause, juggling fire in the middle of our intersection, only a few feet from the little jars embossed with my beautiful face. Why, I wonder, are people okay with *that* but not Wentastic BBQ? What charms do psychopath clowns possess that I don't? And—I think—if the juggler catches on fire, it could be good publicity to douse her with a jar of delicious red sauce.

While Wentastic BBQ makes its silent debut on the anything-goes street fair circuit, the Clown House has become a cottage industry. On previous Last Thursday visits it was always a highlight. Past events included a mud wrestling match that looked like a mime convention in need of a bath…but with whiskey and cigarettes mixed in. Last time, a gang of female clowns in pink tutus showcased a BMX ballet bordering between performance art on two wheels and pornography on two wheels. This clownsanity used to be free of charge, just for kicks and the joy of being at the right place at the right time. Thus, making all the card table salesmen, like myself, happy for the foot traffic.

But today, of course—Wentastic BBQ's capitalistic debut—the clowns demand donations. Cold hard currency. Viewers are now expected to pay when the fire is flying, the eating contest reaches button-popping limits and the surprisingly good all-Caucasian reggae band thumps on stage.

Tonight, it's all about capitalism for the anarchists, too. Why the change in politics? Here's a shocking news flash: communes populated by 20-something slacker clowns can't afford their rent. Apparently, if people don't donate money and help cover the bills, we may never see worthwhile programming like tonight's popular clown-curated skit: *My Burning Baby. My Burning Tricycle. My Burning Mustache.* It's all starting to sound less anarchist and more Public Broadcasting fundraiser.

I can't help but assume some of these donations are stealing dollar bills out of my pocket. These clowns easily raked in more money than Wentastic Enterprises. It couldn't be hard, really. After only selling a few jars and giving away three, the guy peddling tube socks is probably closer to financial independence.

How come?

I think the answer is that greasy bitch economics professors call "credibility." Turns out, when you're trying to score as much money as possible at a lawless street fair, *Street Cred* is the name of the game. Doesn't matter if you're trying to pay the rent or build Trumpian levels of cash via brisket's best friend. Those with the public's trust rule the street, an aspect the Wentastic Enterprises board of directors ignored.

"Starting today, things are gonna change around this office," I will say at the annual Wentastic BBQ shareholders meeting in Aspen. "We're gonna go big time. We're gonna hit the streets and build a buzz. We're gonna burrow our way into America's hearts and flick it behind the ear!" That's where I pound my fist on the long table with a bunch of old guys shivering. "And we're gonna start with a *classy* campaign. Effective immediately, I'm stepping down as the face of this BBQ Sauce." I dramatically rip a label from a bottle. This is the part where the old men gasp. One faints. "I know what the people want. They want credibility. So, from now on we'll have the banjo playing tricycle clown on the labels. Give him a big hand. America loves this guy!"

As you already guessed, stocks begin to soar. Clowns pay their rent. Finally, I retire early.

JUNGLE JUICE

There is one kind of polar bear in Estacada, OR: the asexual kind.

A zoo's polar bear is usually more than 20 feet away, sleeping and—by my best guess—only the size of a St. Bernard. A polar bear in Estacada stands 12 feet tall, a few inches from your nose and is intimidatingly huge.

But this is what we are hunting for this morning. That, and a stiff bloody mary.

Estacada is a dot of town. It's a speck of pepper on Oregon maps. It boasts one gas station, which features a Taco Time restaurant. It is an hour east of Portland and the last sign of humanity before an enormous state park. Amazingly, Estacada also hosts the Safari Club: without a doubt the most bizarre watering hole in America.

Describing its style is tough. African-Apocalypse Chic? Frozen-in-Time Jungle? Embarrassingly Americana? The Safari Club is where you go for a drink, for greasy Chinese food next door and for karaoke singing beneath stuffed cheetahs.

I've heard mutterings of this place since moving to Portland three years ago. Part *Wild Kingdom*, part dive bar, part totally worth the drive. The Safari Club is where big game hunting marries binge drinking and pops out a baby of Elephant Man proportions.

The story goes that the original owner of this tiny bar, Glenn Park, also happened to be the country's foremost safari hunter in the 50s and 60s. Faced with the problem most famous big game warlords encounter—"What to do when your home gets cluttered with stuffed tigers?"—Park fired his rifle into logic's heart and turned his tavern into a taxidermy museum.

Places like the Safari Club give Europeans the impression all Americans own firearms. I'm starting to believe it myself.

We are greeted at the entrance by the aforementioned freaking huge polar bear and his smaller cousin, the Alaskan brown bear. Both are on hind legs, flashing switchblade teeth and claws like fuzzy muggers. Both are the size of economy cars. Sadly, both have a bald spot below their bellies. Their genitalia must have been removed to ensure the Safari Club was suitable for Sunday school field trips.

It is, after all, sort of the Noah's Ark of taxidermy.

These dueling beasts are trapped behind glass. Before them are two handwritten pieces of paper taped to the window. "Restaurant," with an arrow to the right. "Bar," with an arrow to the left. These are positioned so you can't really read the plaques telling where these furry wrecking balls were killed. The monstrous bears are an afterthought, almost as if they are just part of the wallpaper scheme.

This morning, we are hungover from a night of camping and drinking at the state park. This Safari Club visit promises two of life's great hangover cures: bloody marys and stuffed gazelles. We are not disappointed on either front.

A dark hallway leading to an equally night-black lounge is some sort of backwoods natural history museum. Huge, nightmarish African creatures—sleek and tight with muscles—lead our way to vodka, tomato juice and Tabasco. Two Bengal tigers wrestle next to the pool tables, each a hiccup from tearing the other's throat into a tasty snack.

To their left, a leopard, spotted and equally mummified, sits on a plastic rock ready to destroy a daydreaming hyena. A little further down the Tunnel of Taxidermy Love, a gazelle watches over the Oregon Lottery poker machines.

Me, I can barely shuffle my feet, stalking my prey slowly: something strong enough to knock my head back into alignment.

Did I mention the entire building looks like a grass hut? Or at least it did in 1971 when the Safari opened its door. Estacada has a cute downtown as small as the distance between third base and home plate. The buildings are sturdy brick and classic except for the Safari Club. Glenn Park's deadly showroom has a thatched roof that was once painted green but now could at best be called grayish. The highest point in Estacada is the faded Safari Club sign that fails to mention the frozen zoo hell within.

But there's no need for advertisements. It's pretty obvious where all the dead animals hang out in town.

Beyond the pool tables lies the tiny lounge. Antelope busts are shoulder-to-shoulder on the wall. Behind the bar, a massive, wooly black buffalo's head watches us place an order. It dwarfs the bartender's standard, human-sized skull. It's intimidating to sit across from, especially sipping a bloody mary as that hangover tingles our limbs.

I drown out my friends' chatter and try and piece everything together. Why would a man build the Safari Club? Why wouldn't Park just donate these creatures to a museum? Or to a school? Or a haunted house?

I'm supposed to believe Glenn Park flew to Africa, risked possible death to shoot a tiger, sent its corpse back to Spokane, Washington for stuffing (this tidbit was related to me via a weathered, but legible, plaque next to the brown bear) and then organized the entire gang into a make-believe jungle in an Estacada tavern? While, yes, this is a great roadside attraction, there has to be an easier way to sell cocktails on a Sunday morning. Was the World's Largest Aluminum Foil Ball already busy?

Maybe a dense pride pushed the hunter? Perhaps Park was sending a message to the youth of Estacada: "Stay in school, don't do drugs and always clean your rifle after sending giraffes to heaven."

Actually, I decide, the jungle pub is some symbol of a rapidly fading era when we, as Americans, assumed we could kick anything's ass. We used to have so much strength and pride. Now the country just snickers and hopes anything representing strength and pride disappears. Bad memories of virility lost, maybe.

No matter what fueled Park's bloody quest, it is, easily, the most brilliant anti-theft device in history. Robbery rates would plummet if bank and liquor store proprietors showcased rhinos they bagged. I would wager a hundred gazelle pelts that the Safari Club has never been held up. Most likely, the criminal element knows somewhere near the cash register lies a rifle large enough to carve a porthole through an elephant.

Aside from the dueling neutered bears, the centerpiece of the Safari Club is the dance floor and stage. The bartender says they host bands once a month and karaoke on the weekends. This makes me incredibly sad, as it has always been a dream to drunkenly sing Huey Lewis' "Power of Love" on a stage with a thatched roof while two pouncing cheetahs leap out above me with frozen snarls, bragging: "I Break for Human Meat."

The Safari's weak coffee and eyeball-popping drinks are bringing life to our taxidermied brains, but don't fully do the trick. My mind is stuck while the souls of exotic animals float in and out of the room. I ask myself why men build any of the roadside crap in this country. What makes someone whittle a maze into a cornfield or advertise the world's smallest bicycle?

Is this only an American thing?

Is there an Indonesian equivalent to the Mystery Spot? More importantly, what makes six American kids roll out of their tents with Hiroshima-sized headaches just to down bloody marys amongst stuffed teddy bears?

After a few more sip-and-cringe sessions with my 100-proof bloody mary, I realize the answer. It's simple. Turns out, we are cut from the same leather as Glenn Park.

We're hunters, too.

There's a burn in our bellies (which might just be acid reflux) to track down and execute our hangovers. We hunted hangovers using stiff bloody marys and Chinese takeout as weapons. We're standing over their carcasses. We want to nail these aches and regrets to the wall like a 50-pound marlin.

Slurping my glass until there's nothing left but a puddle of ice and tomato gunk, I feel much better—more human. Not quite as strong and proud as days gone, but I feel a little bit like Mr. Glenn Park.

Maybe it's the entertaining decorations. Maybe it's the slight morning buzz. But most likely it's the satisfaction of neutering this hangover like a bear penis.

I'VE DIED AND GONE TO TEXAS

My first thought after rolling into the parking lot is: "Holy crap, I've died and gone to Texas." This comes seconds after Tim and I sweep our jaws off the ground, watching a man load an M-16 assault rifle into his trunk like a sack of groceries.

We park the car while firearms of all calibers fall out of the sky. A couple guys lug muskets over their shoulders. A father carries an Army surplus box of ammunition in each hand as his kids skip behind. One fella bullshits with his buddy while swinging a handgun the size of a hairdryer.

This is the Second Amendment launched from a cannon. This, I guess, could be any parking lot from Amarillo to Houston—some alternate dimension where firearms are as common as BBQ stains on shirtfronts.

The weird thing is, it's not. It's tree-hugging Oregon. Specifically, the Portland International Gun and Knife Show. Shockingly, bulletproof vest not required.

A few months back, Tim, our buddy Dan and I forced a coworker to take us shooting. I'd never fired a gun before, but quickly learned it's as addictive as crystal meth. Here's a quick fact: **guns are cool**. If you don't agree, you've obviously never fired one of these steel beauties...or you're Canadian.

I realize I may be making a mistake when I get dressed this afternoon and take an extra second to wonder, "what's a proper gun show outfit?" I'm still new, I don't own any camouflage or work boots. God, I don't even chew SKOAL Bandit. As a dorky kid from the city with a new hard-on for weaponry, I might as well crawl into an elk costume because either way I'm coming home laced with bullet holes.

I'm worried because gun shows have nasty reputations as flea markets for firepower. Hundreds of independent sellers cramming together buying, selling and trading anything from slingshots to bazookas. All the while, charging dirt cheap prices and magically dancing around the Brady Bill.

"Whoa," Tim says as we walk through the Expo Center entrance. His blue eyes blimp enormous. "That dude was loading a revolver back there in the smoking area. Did you see that?" I take a deep breath and pay at the door, knowing behind the turnstile lies a convention center soupy with big game hunters, gang members, postal workers and Republicans—certain death for certain nerds like me.

The red hand stamp is even shaped like a tiny Beretta handgun. Make no mistake, folks, visitors have one thing on their minds.

Sadly, Tim and I don't have the same things on our minds.

Well, not totally. Don't get me wrong, there are lots of guns and knives and samurai swords. Mostly guns: cowboy guns, Uzis, shotguns, Dirty Harry revolvers, Yugoslavian army rifles with bayonets. You name it. It's all yours for a fistful of cash.

But with all this potential madness, I'm quickly disappointed. While I imagined a convention center populated with Unibombers, almost every visitor gives the impression of sanity. They're anyone you'd meet at the mall. Moms and dads and kids and grandpas all inspecting firing chambers laid out across sterile tables. This might as well be *Antiques Roadshow*. They could be scrutinizing Faberge eggs. No disgruntled letter carriers, no beer burping militiamen, nobody even the slightest bit fidgety.

Tim and I are the closest thing to irresponsible, gun-obsessed wackos.

Here's another fact. Guns are cool, but when not exploding in your hand and terrorizing watermelons, guns are really boring. They just quietly sit there like all those unterrorized watermelons at the store. Except chained to a table.

I don't plan to buy a peacemaker, so my eyes glaze over and turn to egg yolks after an hour of staring at Dick Cheney's wet dream. Tim, on the other hand, is convinced gun ownership is in his future. He was a Thai Boy Scout, I guess it's natural.

It takes next-to-no-time to figure out how soggy gun shows are. The interesting bits about the gun show deal very little with actual firearm sales. It's the people and the idiosyncrasies that bring this 40-caliber snore fest to life.

Here's a cliff notes version of those interesting things:

WWI Dude is a young guy, no more than 21, marching around the convention center wearing a faded green field sweater, knee-high canvas pants, thick boots and a little brown army hat with an infantry rifle at his shoulder. As far as I can tell he isn't there to buy anything, just guarding the perimeter from Germans.

Speaking of Germans, **Nazi Memorabilia Guy** has his swastika flag flying high. Luckily, no skirmishes break out between the two. That's not hard to imagine, since the old guy selling Third Reich Medals for $450 and framed Hitler photos for $15, looks more like Waylon Jennings' bass player than a bloodthirsty goosestepper.

Surprisingly, **children** are well represented. For every three people buying ammo there is a gunpowder-hungry tyke begging to hold his first Colt. One lucky buckaroo in a stroller is pushed around as dad dangles a pistol from his belt like he's the sheriff of Tombstone. This guy also decided to use the stroller as a gun rack—storing a long hunting rifle in the pouch usually reserved for frivolous perks like Pampers and Similac.

Another interesting kiddie piece is a tiny .22 caliber rifle with a cartoon bug on the box wearing a smile and neon orange hunting vest. This birthday surprise is adorably called "Davey Cricket—My first Rifle."

My theory about being too dorky for the Gun Show is proven true by the **Book Sale**. These tomes are a million times more exotic than the firepower around me. It makes sense, really. If someone wants to find a gun, they can just go down to their nearest grade school. But visit Borders and see if you can find any gun show books. Titles include: *Advanced Homemade Fireworks, Backyard Ballistics, Sniper Techniques, Thank God I Had a Gun, Hand-to-Hand Combat, The Mac-10 Cookbook* and *Poor Man's James Bond*. I purchase the Army issued 1967 field manual, *Boobytraps*. If you ever need to construct an effective tripwire or exploding bunk bed, I'm your man.

Oddly, amongst all the instructional texts on killing people with your hands is *Fondue and Hot Dips*. A little something for the ladies.

But that isn't all for gunmen's wives. You have to look hard, but amongst all the rifles, right next to the guy selling bayonets, is a cute old woman wearing a denim shirt embroidered with neon cats. Here you can quench your Beanie Baby fix. And while you're at it, buy one of her hand-stitched dishtowels with hunting rifles and automatic weapons on them.

Sadly, this cookie-baking wuss wouldn't last more than 10 seconds in a steel cage with the granny at the other end of the show. Here, a gentle elderly woman sells crossbows and nunchucks, wearing a hand-scrawled nametag reading: "Life is Good." No wonder organizers separated these two estrogen camps. If not, there'd be nothing but a pile of dishtowel fuzz and Beanie guts left at the end of the day.

But no, they didn't meet one another. God-forbid something interesting actually happen here.

The only true scare is the mandatory waiting period. Whether purchasing a $100 Davey Cricket or the $60,000 anti-tank blaster, every salesman must perform a background check.

Forcing myself to build a little journalistic integrity, I decide to do some research. Lifting a heavy black machine gun—the kind you'd split a guy in half with playing Nintendo—I ask the merchant: "So, say I had…" I check the price tag: *Holy shit, flaming death is cheap*, I think. "$475 today and wanted to take this assault rifle home and… do stuff with it. What would happen?"

"Well," the friendly and incredibly sane gun salesman says. He takes a moment to rub his hands on his plaid shirt. "I'd copy your driver's license and have you fill out a form."

"What's on the form?"

"We just ask if you're a citizen, if you're a drug addict, if you're a felon…that kind of stuff."

"And what if I answer all that…correctly?" I say massaging this black steel monster like it needs a backrub. "Then what?"

"Uh, well, I call the police and they do a quick background check and if everything clears, you can take that baby home."

Aiming the barrel at the ceiling, looking through the sight, I say: "How long does all this take? You know, how soon can I take it home…and do *stuff* with it?"

"Oh, no more than ten, fifteen minutes."

This shoots Freon up my spine and makes me want to wear a

bulletproof vest the rest of my life. Machine gun ownership is faster than a dental cleaning.

Walking back to the car we laugh, waving to a cop as we carry a British infantry rifle and a hunting rifle Tim bought with $150 and a clean criminal record. You feel like you're getting away with something, even though it's perfectly legal. There is the surprise of the day...the unexpected pleasure.

We walked up to the gun show expecting every redneck cliché in the book and came out looking a little closer to that vision than anybody in attendance. It turns out gun people aren't crazy. Trigger fingers don't make fringe outlaws anymore. Like thousands of other people that come to the Expo Center every year—stamp collectors or cat fanciers, for example—they're just boring Americans with a hobby.

And so I leave in a soft funk.

Once again, organization has clipped and painted the last wild toenail of something once dangerous and thrilling in this country. Order and lawfulness has gentrified another mystery.

But I'm not telling that to Waylon Jennings' bass player.

MARY LOU RETTON'S BLADDER RUINED THE STATE FAIR

Olympic gymnast and 80s icon Mary Lou Retton tells a crowd she has to take a piss every minute of the day and it becomes clear: The State Fair is the saddest place on earth.

The State Fair has, for years, been a symbol of all things American. It's where your fellow citizens come together and salute their flag, ride tilt-a-whirls and judge beauty pageants for teenage girls and Holsteins alike. On a good day, it's where everyone learns something new about home and eats something fried. It's a place where hard-working carnies hold your life in their heavily tattooed hands.

It's not the place we come to see how American culture is stepping on its own neck. It's definitely not the place we come to hear a midget with a gold medal discuss her bladder.

The Oregon State Fair held a lot of promise. This state is weird and I assumed this would be some sort of Nutjob State of the Union. Hell, the Fair's commercial involved Donald Duck (The University of Oregon's mascot), a Sasquatch and the blonde dude who sang in Everclear cruising down the highway in a convertible. This was a big freak flag and it looked to me like it was flying high over Salem.

It wasn't until we were in the parking lot when my wife reminded me that Portland is the only wacky place in Oregon. The rest of the state is very rural and fairly conservative. She had a great point, but I didn't let it slow down my lust for one-eyed carnival workers, pie baking contests and America's sweetheart, Mary Lou Retton.

In a one-two punch that seemed like proof to its oddness, Friday's big draw was American redneck supreme Ted Nugent. This afternoon offered everyone's aforementioned favorite gymnastic legend. I assumed Mary Lou would perform some floor routines and maybe even a number on the uneven bars, tell us to stay in school and cartwheel out the door to the beat of hammering applause. In the meantime, I planned on having a love-in with our delicious state fish, the salmon, and poke the ferris wheel operator with a stick to hear him growl about how, "This town ain't no Sacramento."

Man, was I wrong.

By now, everyone's heard endless white noise about this dying economy and the American way of life are, well, *killing* the American way of life. While I agree with a lot of that, I'm not going to preach. I *will* however sermonize about how fiscal bedlam and the American way of life are killing my beloved State Fair.

Things start off fairly promising as my wife and I walk through a maze of old rides clanking and screeching and birthing vomit. Further down the path, we're boxed in by the usual array of shooting/tossing carnival games. But we didn't come for the rides and games. We are adults now and, damn it, we've come for mature things like bearded ladies.

The first fair-like thing we see is a lonely trailer that claims to house a 13-foot alligator. Somehow even the dollar asking price seems a little steep, so we pass. Bigger fish to fry, I tell myself. Next is an elaborate booth provided by the Highway Patrol about crystal meth. While it is meant to scare kids, it more or less gives step-by-step directions for how to cook meth in their basement. Oddly, right next to this, the Highway Patrol offers a game which boils down to, "Guess which roadkill's fur is which!" I don't see the connection, which must mean I'll never cut it as a radar gun jockey.

Things pick up steam in the State Fair pavilion with, "The Great American Spam Championship." Here, a representative from the canned meat king accepts recipes; the winner gets theirs on a can of Spam. While the judging takes place, he and his assistant play 20 Questions of Spam. This consists of, "Can anyone tell me how many cans of Spam it would take to equal the weight of the Statue of Liberty?" A man in the front row has the highest guess with a billion, while I have the lowest at seven. The truth is somewhere around 70 million. The winner gets a t-shirt.

We also learn on your 30th anniversary working at Spam you

don't get a gold watch, but your likeness carved in gooey pink meat. Wow. "This," I start to think, "is what America is all about."

I look at the rest of the schedule and see our little gymnastic dynamo is sandwiched between the Home Depot Tool Contest and the Hermiston Watermelon Seed Spitting Championship.

I start to feel embarrassed. This woman was the first athlete on the front of a Wheaties box and now she's second banana to seed-spitters? Where's the justice?

Adding salt to my rapidly opening sores, the brochure says she's here to talk about taking charge of your health. I'm disappointed there will be no pommel horse, but decide it's probably a good topic since everyone is eating elephant ears and deep fried Snickers bars. Sadly, I didn't read the fine print beneath her photo.

I'm starting to suspect my wife is right: the Oregon State Fair isn't a haven for the Beaver State's weirdoes. The remainder of the pavilion is filled with the 4-H baking competition, and it's safe to assume these brownies aren't *special*. There's a cake decorating contest, some kid's pocket knife collection (at 77, while impressive, I fail to see how this earned its own booth), a quilting bee, a dress making contest (I actually get a little burst of hope when one of the entries is made of Duct Tape!) and possibly the world's most boring exhibit: The Oregon Table Setting Competition. Yep, you guessed it, a contest to see who can put the salad fork in the right place.

We leave the pavilion kind of wondering why we paid to see this. Though, I now have a new goal in life: to be an official 2007 Oregon State blueberry pie judge.

The rest of the fair goes nowhere but downhill and in a tilt-a-whirl-type hurry. My wife delivers another dose of common sense: "The fair is a place you pay to get in so you can pay for more shit." Everyone is selling stuff, from chickens to dairy cows to cheap t-shirts to farm equipment to gourmet wine. This is starting to look like Oregon's Largest Swap Meet...with a fried food court.

If the food court at the State Fair doesn't make you seasick, you are a culinary pirate. It's exactly what I expect: lots of overweight Americans eating things that shouldn't be fried. *This, I start to think, is what America is all about.* I'm always interested to see how far the carnival pushes the culinary envelope every year. Corndogs and elephant ears are old news. They're grandma's fair food. A few years ago stomachs ached across this country when an industrious carny deep fried a Twinkie and sold it for four bucks. I'm psyched to see what's new.

What catches me this year, aside from the Ketchup Udder—a ketchup and mustard dispenser that works like a cow udder—is the MONSTER Fry Brick. For five bucks some dirty chef fills an entire deep fry basket full of French fries. By this, I mean they pack it full of potatoes until it's a solid block. Then they dunk it in scalding oil. What comes out is a crispy yellow tater loaf.

The family beside our picnic table sits down with a brick. The wife and I quietly eat the only light thing available, a chicken skewer with rice (surprisingly, not fried rice) and a coconut shaved ice. Normally, I wouldn't be embarrassed about this but at the state fair eating healthy is like having communist leanings in the 50s. The Wensinks should be blacklisted. I assume at any moment the Carny CIA will take us away and force feed me chilidogs. Before we leave, our patriotic neighbors order another MONSTER Fry Brick.

God bless you, patriots.

After lunch I start to chip away at the carny illusion at the Oregon State Fair. And, if we're shooting for a sociology project, what's happening to this country in general. Yes, it's becoming fat, but America's also being ruined by efficiency. The proof, you ask? Funtastic Traveling Shows.

I practically go into seizure when I realize all the carny booths are painted the same orange. None of the workers have facial scars or tattoos or prosthetic limbs. Every ticket taker is well-groomed and clean…and worst of all, wearing uniforms.

I'm fine with a Starbucks on every corner and Time Warner owning pretty much everything else. Every consumable product in America can be traced back to five or six parent corporations. Whatever. That's acceptable…at least it was before this mentality crept into my beloved State Fair.

Funtastic's slogan, "Quite Possibly…the World's Finest Carnival," is their corporate rally cry. It says, "No more independent carnies. No more bearded ladies. No more grizzly, smoking pedophiles running the Tilt-A-Whirl."

The noble carny is the last pioneer, the final nomad of this quickly shrinking nation. They go from town to town, don't give a damn about anything and feed you fried goodies. They're heroes. They are what's great about America. And like every other brilliant aspect of this country, someone figured out how to turn a profit by draining all the character out. Funtastic has its fingers around the carnies' throats and it's not afraid to squeeze.

My mouth is sour after noticing this. The same kids that work at Forever 21, now encourage you to shoot water into a clown's mouth. I'm in a horribly sweaty place and only one person can save my day—1984 Women's Gymnastics All-Around Gold Medalist: you know who.

Sadly, the Oregon State Fair, already staggering around like a now-unemployed, drunken one-legged bumper car operator, comes crashing down back in the pavilion. On the same stage where I dreamed about having my face carved out of salty, canned meat, Ms. Retton stands.

She's tiny. I could easily squish her into a French fry basket and cook a MONSTER Lou Retton. She still has the growth-stunted voice of an 11-year-old. And she's not here to stress the importance of the food pyramid or how staying away from drugs is cool.

In fact, she's here selling drugs.

Mary Lou's now a representative for corporatized, All-American, pharmaceutical behemoth Pfizer. If Funtastic Traveling Shows sold medication, it would be called Pfizer.

Little Mary Lou doesn't even have the courtesy to slip into a leotard, speaking into the mic wearing a business suit. She never jumps or spins or flips. She just wraps her life story into a well-rehearsed drug commercial.

Mary suffers from an overactive bladder. Her whole life—even while whipping Russian ass at the Olympics—she's had to piss really bad. It caused a lot of anxiety and suffering over the years. But now, thanks to her friends (and sugar daddies) at Pfizer, she is no longer a slave to her urine. She's working on a campaign called, "Life Beyond the Bathroom" and is encouraging people to come out of the water closet to admit that they, too, need to pee.

Pissed off and sad, Leah and I leave before she's done. Mary Lou has thrown the last shovelful of dirt on the State Fair's grave. The annual celebration of Oregon's awesomeness is ruined.

We're paying money to spend money.

And even when we're not spending money, we're being sold corporate urine medicine from an American hero. Now I realize the seed spitting contest is sponsored by a watermelon producer. The Spam Championship is a fancy, traveling commercial. Who knows… the 13-foot alligator is probably paid for by Sea World.

Not even the Tilt-A-Whirl can bring a smile to our faces, especially since the operator's never spent the night in county jail, let alone capital-P Prison. There is no uncharted corporate territory. "This," I tell myself, "is what America is all about."

America's all about getting gross in tough times. Apparently you can't write "Pro Gymnast" on your taxes, even if you add a smiley face. So, American icons also need to work degrading jobs these days. American efficiency at its scariest again.

But still, staring this evil money machine in the eyes, we have to laugh. Any company that gives away free Post-Its that say "LifeBeyondtheBathroom.com" at least has a sense of humor, right?

LIVE LONGER, MISMATCH YOUR SOCKS

"What will people *think*?" Mom asked, many years ago, looking at my ankles in a panic.

She denies it now, but I can't forget. I was speechless because it never occurred to me anyone was paying attention.

Turns out, people have a lot to say about a man's sock choice. It's just nobody mentions it until they finally match.

I gave up matching my socks almost 10 years ago. One day, in our crummy apartment in Portland, I just stopped seeing the point. There was never any intended fashion statement. Though, I guess, people could see it that way. Probably because, in addition to refusing to ball socks together, I also wore colorful patterns.

So, when I sported a blue argyle clashed against a red wool, nobody said a word. I just assumed coworkers and friends simply didn't notice. Socks were safely hidden under my pants. It wasn't like I was wearing Birkenstocks and volleyball shorts. I went along blindly filling my sock drawer until it looked like the Laundromat lost and found.

On rare occasions—like weddings or a Russian-Roulette-like chance that the two I pulled out were brothers—I wore matching socks. And only then did everyone let me know they were, in fact, paying very close attention.

"Hey, your socks match!"

"Whoa, what gives?"

"Finally gave up that weird sock stuff, huh?"

I grew incredibly self-conscious, like a spy movie when everyone is clandestinely watching the main character. But, by that point, I wore my socks with pride. I knew I'd live a more fulfilling life than any of my critics.

How?

Simple math. The only kind of math I know.

Let's say you spend five minutes, once a week, matching socks. No big loss, right? Meanwhile, I dump my socks into a drawer without another moment's thought.

You repeat this task 52 times a year. That's nearly four-and-a-half hours a year!

"Worth it, for ankular symmetry," you say.

I'll be generous and guess you'll live to be 75. You look feisty. That, my fashion conscious chum, adds up to a tidy 14 days. Two weeks over your lifetime!

With an extra pair of weeks one could learn to ski. One could travel to sockless locales like Fiji. One could fall in love.

Or…one could make sure that the beige sock and the tan sock are properly separated. Thank god.

Keep matching socks if you like. Just don't come crying to me when you're 75 and wishing you had just a couple more weeks to spend with your grandkids. I won't be listening. Me and my clash-footed family will be skiing in Fiji, charming the pants off the natives.

WENTASTIC GUIDE TO AVOIDING WORK

"My opinion…" the doctor said, holding little mountain range EKG readings. "It's called holiday heart."

"Okay," I said. But actually thought: *This is her way of softening me up. I am having a heart attack. I am 28 and dying of coronary failure. I should think of something awesome for my tombstone.*

"The name comes from people getting this way around family holidays. Whenever you mix binge drinking and stress, heart arrhythmias arise."

It was August. Nowhere near a holiday. My family was 2000 miles away.

"So what does that mean?" My left arm wasn't numb or anything. But I'd been having dull pains in my chest for a week. I was thoroughly freaked enough to call the doctor. Fortunately, she said I wasn't showing any signs of heart attack or stroke or other aortic oogie-boogies. Despite what my night sweats and bad dreams were telling me, I was a healthy man. Death was not penciled in my date book just yet.

"Cut back on your drinking and cut back on your stress," she said. "Come back in a couple weeks if it's not better."

The drinking I could cut back on. I knocked back more than enough to make a horse lose its balance, sure. But, it wasn't like I started shaking without a beer.

The stress, though, was going to be tougher. I'm one of those people who gets in a hurry and swallows all the stress in a nasty coil at the dead center of his chest. Anxiety was magnetized to my body and growing and seemingly trying to eat me alive.

I've had a rotten relationship with work. I hated jobs and jobs, apparently, hated me.

Proof:

Saint Patrick's Day 2004—I'm a part-time marketing assistant at a children's museum here in Portland. At least I was until my boss calls a surprise meeting and says she's firing me. Her reason for cutting me loose on the **DAY I'M NAMED FOR**: *"It's just not a good fit."*

I'd only been there since January and hadn't heard any complaints until this point. Result: pack your desk into a cardboard box and get escorted out while nosy parents wonder if I'm some sort of child molester. Which is a valid question. Honestly, who gets fired from a children's museum?

Two Days Before Christmas 2004—Still surfing a nasty skid of unemployment from the above firing, I'm working a temp gig entering data for a life insurance company. This time I get, "We're going to have to ask you not to come into the office anymore." This is the result of reminding my boss that I've had plane tickets to visit my family for the holidays for nearly three months. I would be taking a few days off, unpaid. This doesn't waltz with her plans of me only taking Christmas day off and then returning to the number-crunch-factory until my 10-key hand falls off. Result: pack your desk into a cardboard box and don't steal any of the decorations, mister. It's Christmas.

The Day Precisely between Christmas and New Years 2006—Preemptively quitting a legal assistant job at the public defender's office, I'm told my two weeks notice isn't necessary and that I need to leave immediately. Some sort of quasi-quitting/quasi-firing. I had to bring in my union rep just to get the two week's pay and insurance I was owed. Things got ugly, HR reps phoned me. Voices were raised.

My current cause of employment anxiety stemmed from a yearlong stint proofreading life insurance documents. Much like the other jobs, I hated this one. Not in that cute, "is it Friday yet?" way of coffee mugs and *Dilbert* cartoons. We're talking a strong phobia. We're talking a gravitational pull toward hell as soon as I walked in the door. Due to doctor's orders and this existential angina, I invented several creative ways of dealing with stress at work.

The Mama Cass

[Yes, it's an urban legend she died feeding her sadness with ham sandwiches. Just play along, okay?]

This one is easiest because it simply means plugging an emotional hole with something else. I didn't invent this idea. I'm pretty sure heart-sick housewives with a taste for Swiss chocolate and pool boys did. And for that, I tip my hat, ladies.

My vice was a record collection. A massive, bloated, senseless record collection. We're talking several hundred vinyl albums and over a thousand CDs. And this was not a good thing. Because, while I'd like everyone to think it was filled with Tchaikovsky albums and rare bootlegs of Lou Reed playing a zither the bulk of its flab were record geek novelties like Bill Cosby's singing attempt.

There are no jokes on 1967's *Silver Throat*. Instead, Rudy and Theo's dad wanders through some clumsy R&B numbers and a fairly cool reworking of Stevie Wonder's "Uptight." That particular tune requires some deep listening, but delivers subtly strong commentary on race relations.

But this song's value was no excuse. I shouldn't have owned that album. Nobody but Cosby's mom should really own *Silver Throat*. And yet, there it was. The album was used at Everyday Music for two bucks. I just piled it onto the stack and hoped visions of a swift death at the copier would disappear.

I experienced countless moments like this. I seem to remember a particularly wicked obsession with acquiring all the Grifters' singles. "Okay, dude's a fan of sloppy 90s Memphis rock," you'd say. And you'd be wrong. While I own their albums, I can't stand to listen to them. I also own three Esquivel records. Short of a misguided music major trying to look "worldly," people are really throwing money away by owning more than one Esquivel record.

And yet, there it was. And it felt good at the time. I needed it.

Much like a children's cough medicine addiction or phobia of monkeys throwing feces, this wasn't my fault. This bulging album collection was the fault of my job.

I'd never found work that suited me. Since graduating six years earlier at the brink of the US's financial toilet wretch, I'd never done anything I was trained for. I was wearing down quickly.

"Who needs the entire catalog of that band that sang 'Mexican Radio?'" you would sensibly ask. A guy who'd run out of options killing time at work, that's who. The guy with mysterious stabbing pains in his chest usually associated with turkey dinners and humiliating uncles. That guy needed help. He *needed* Wall of Voodoo.

This sad coping technique was no better than the homeless guys I'd step over on the way to the record store. They were curled up on a cardboard mat, itching at strip mined arms and scheming where next to get a spoonful of help. Me, I was stuffed into a pair of khaki pants, itching to get out of a windowless cubicle, surfing the internet for musical inspiration toward my next fix.

I was a mainliner. I couldn't stop myself. I was like the singer of INXS at a beatoff contest, but with records. Sure, some I was genuinely excited about, but most albums I only partially wanted— if at all. Many weeks, I spent over $100 on records. I'd buy them two and three at a time, hopscotching to various shops. And a wave of calm would stretch across my skin for a little while.

After sitting at my cubicle in the morning, thinking about going to the record store at lunch was all that got me through meetings about better editing techniques for accidental death and dismemberment forms. And then in the afternoon, either putting my CD into the computer or dreaming about dropping the vinyl on the turntable at home kept me sane through endless post-lunch phone calls from people demanding help reformatting form C-45-B-10007.

Like the pioneer medical cure of rubbing butter on a burn, it seemed like it should help but only made things hurt worse.

I was spending so much time compiling lists of albums to buy—I once heard "Bottle of Wine" by the Fireballs on the radio and, for reasons now unknown, became obsessed with tracking down the entire Fireballs discography [I also did the same thing with the guy who sang "Take a Letter, Maria." These were dark times, folks]—that my work suffered. Thus, making it even more stressful to be at the insurance company. And, obviously, contributing to my chest pains.

Somewhere a snake was dining on its tail.

Like good after-school specials teach us, this was a gateway. Soon records weren't enough to eliminate my desire to jump down an elevator shaft in an oxford cloth shirt. Between record hunts I was doing everything I could to pull the release valve off the little pressure cooker in my chest.

The Secret Agent

One popular method I perfected was reading books on the toilet. I'd mastered this delicate art years earlier at my first post-college, non-busboy job as an administrative assistant at a nonprofit in Tucson. [Proud to say I quit and was not fired!]

The trick, like with all time-wasters, was to remain inconspicuous. Offices large and small are hives of watching eyes. Gossip is just as good as buying Cosby records to some. So, getting spotted carrying a book to the bathroom wasn't a conversation I wanted to have. "Hey, Patrick, there a lending library in the Men's now? Ha, ha, ha." Books would get me noticed and labeled a slacker and therefore more closely monitored…thus making it impossible to slack.

Somewhere, a snake was slathering itself in mustard between a hotdog bun.

Paperbacks were the key. Hardback books need not apply.

Why?

Simple. Paperbacks form-fit to one's ankle. And a nice, tight sock could be pulled over that book to hold it in place. Loose khaki slacks dropped over this covert little bundle of literature, obscuring it from wandering eyes.

The second key: Nice easy steps. That book threatened to fall out at any second and it very well could've, so it was crucial to take comfortable steps that didn't jostle the ankle. Nobody wants a book slingshotting from their pantleg. It sends messages that most offices aren't equipped to decode.

I read Johnny Cash's autobiography, among others, atop the toilet on company time. And it made me feel like James Bond. Anytime you can make yourself seem more spy-like, you've already kicked anxiety in the nuts.

But no amount of books-on-crappers could fully remove the stress. I couldn't duck into the toilet for eight hours a day. So, the next method involved looking like work was being done while accomplishing nothing.

The Shell Game

Some jerks think they can get away with clicking off a non-work website when they hear footsteps approaching. This method of slacking begs for trouble next time an office ballerina silently pirouettes past.

The Shell Game was the only way to go and it was even tougher than the literary ankle holster. It required, first and foremost, an employer that used file folders. Jobs I held at the insurance company and a public defender's office were perfect for this. So were a variety of temp jobs. Basically, I only needed a stack of physical paperwork. Why?

Because I covertly printed online movie reviews, lengthy *New York Times* articles and whole rambling Wikipedia pages—the same internet stuff you'd try to sneak in anyway—while printing off actual work.

With hours-worth of online surfage on paper, it was easily slipped into file folders of actual work and inspected like I was focusing really hard on new life insurance policies. Meanwhile, I was learning about Wikipedia's fascinating history of sea monsters.

I also used this time to edit an entire novel, 15 pages at a time. This made it look like I was red-inking the hell out of some offending insurance document.

If you added all this wasted time up, it's amazing I accomplished anything work-related. And yet, there it was—the stress and pain. My heart exploding like a holiday.

I'd only worked the insurance job about 18 months and already it was killing me. My stress chest was a baby grand with wires pulled tight. Things were ready to snap.

I was begging for someone to go Jerry Lee Lewis in *Great Balls of Fire* and dump a bottle of whiskey in this piano and toss in a match. A cardiovascular Molotov cocktail.

And then, with my productivity skidding to its inevitable trickle, what with reading an oral history about the first dog in space, I was called into the boss' cubicle. Which, by the way, was identical to my own cube except it had a window. So, as if I needed motivation, another 30 years of time-wasting in the life insurance biz would earn me a blinding midday view of another skyscraper. Hooray.

This chat came hot on the heels of a discussion about my

appearance. In corporate America, supervisors cannot tell someone to trim their beard at least once a fortnight or comb their hair or wear clothes that didn't come from a thrift store. That conversation has discrimination lawsuit written all over it. So, managers used their own James Bond role playing in other ways. They'd say: "Pat, don't you want to look presentable? Don't you want department heads to admire how sharp you can dress? Don't you think it'd make a good impression on everyone?"

Our final chat was not about grooming, however. The pear-shaped woman in charge of all the other insurance form gurus had a lot to say. I'm not really clear anymore what nuggets she passed along. Frankly, I was busy daydreaming about sea monsters. The gist, from my memory, was "your productivity has *really* fallen," "you're making a *lot* of mistakes," "if I don't see an improvement, we are going to have to investigate *other options*."

Other options, for those not in on the lingo, meant I could read books on the toilet at my house because I would be unemployed again.

Well, that was about all I needed to hear. I'm sure my boss hoped this would spark some enthusiastic fervor for editing short term disability brochures, but it did not. It, frankly, made said existential angina burn in the most depressingly hot manner possible.

Not even a novelty Cosby record would save me. The stressful wires in my chest were getting tighter. They'd built a grenade and were angry. Lights were strobbing and red alert sirens were sounding. It was entirely possible I'd be dead or fired or both in a very short amount of time.

But soon, my need for records slowed. I eventually lost that craving for obscure Van Dyke Parks albums or the Clinic rarities CD that I didn't really need, because, frankly, all Clinic records sound the same.

Soon, I would be enjoying my literature in an armchair like the rest of the world.

Soon, I'd be reading about sea monsters via computer screen, the way nature intended.

You see, somewhere a snake was finishing eating its own tail. Work wanted me gone and I wanted to be gone. The solution was much simpler than I imagined.

I just resigned.

I'd recently been rejected from a slew of MFA programs, so my wife and I were planning a cross country move to Louisville instead of school. However, we lacked the proper motivation to pack up. She was unemployed and the potential of me earning a third firing from a job in Portland pretty much sealed that deal.

So we loaded up the car. And those nasty coils of holiday stress around my heart cooled and went normal. I discovered a way to make a living as a freelance writer and learned all the coping mechanisms in the world can't help when you're truly unhappy...no matter how many fascinating stories there are about that first mutt in space. That unhappiness simply finds a way to burrow through to your core and, without drastic measures, that shit'll kill you.

I keep Cosby's *Silver Throat* album lying around, unplayed, as a reminder to keep my heart calm.

I WAS A KFC TASTE-TESTER

I once felt like a shoo-in for a job. The newspaper where I freelanced as a rock critic had an opening for an assistant music editor. I'd written for the paper for years. I knew my stuff in the music world. Best of all, I was close friends with the head music editor.

I practically had new business cards printed up that day.

However, after applying and waiting, the publisher called and said they were going in another direction.

I pointed out that I was more than qualified.

She agreed.

"So, why, then?" I said.

"We're not looking for a music person, per se."

"You don't want a music fan to fill the assistant music editor position?"

"Exactly! So glad you understand," she said and quickly ended the call.

I cancelled my business card order and savored the flavor of fresh blood in my mouth. I'd just taken a punch from our national obsession with revisionism. But it wasn't my last.

We recently moved to Louisville. Here, it's impossible to ignore Kentucky Fried Chicken.

The restaurant is headquartered right off the highway in a big mansion the same creamy shade as the Colonel's suits. Our basketball arena is named for KFC's parent company. Hell, the chicken giant once offered to fill the city's potholes as long as each had their logo spray painted onto the asphalt.

In addition, there are whispers around about an Area 51-like

Kentucky Fried Test Lab and even softer mumbles that they *pay* tasters.

Rarely are free lunch rumors true. Even rarer are instances of getting paid to dine when you are not a Japanese hotdog eating champion. Against all odds, these rumors were true. After enduring a marathon SAT-style barrage of questions pertaining to restaurant preferences, food preferences, and everything short of my underwear color, I was in. I'd actually taken this phone test twice before and somehow failed. "Congratulations, you'll be tasting Monday. The pay is twenty-dollars," the phone interrogator said.

Free food and free money? This looked suspiciously like one of those deals where the devil pops out of a closet with some paperwork for me to initial and sign.

As a freelance writer, I earned about as much as a paperboy with no aim. I had no problem selling my soul to the Colonel.

A few days later, I was in the center ring of this clucking Thunderdome: the YUM! Brands taste test facility. Oddly, located in the basement of the headquarters' mansion. Inside, the facility looked like anything but the Palace that Poultry Built. There were a few men and women in lab coats taking our names and checking drivers' licenses. The waiting area was reminiscent of temp agencies I'd worked for, but with vintage Colonel Sanders portraits. My tasting time was 11am on a Monday. So, the group consisted of me and a room full of white-haired folks, because, as most people already know, writers and retirees are the only ones with nothing to do on Monday mornings.

"Welcome to your taste test," one lab-coated man said. He had a fluffy mustache and long grey hair tucked under a *Kentucky Grilled Chicken* hat. He sounded as enthused as a button-pusher at Space Mountain. "Today, you will be tasting Long John Silvers' chicken strips…"

Wait just a minute, pal, I thought, but soon stopped myself. KFC is not just KFC, but part of a conglomerate including Pepsi, Pizza Hut, Taco Bell, A&W and, obviously, Long John Silver's. Together, this gang forms a fast food hydra head approaching organizational levels of messiness not seen since I tried counting the colors in George Clinton's hair.

"Also," our supervisor said, "you will have an option to test hushpuppies after the chicken."

Optional Hushpuppies?

Optional Hushpuppies.

Optional Hushpuppies!

Not only are those the two most important words in Harvard's dress code, but they are also the two favorite words of writers and retirees.

We elderly food adventurers and writers were ushered into the testing room that looked like…a temp agency…but with a chromed-out kitchen. We sat at computer monitors and were asked a series of questions regarding our political views of deep fried bird meat.

At this point I was extremely anxious. What insane chicken concoction would be thrown my way? Remember, this is the company that eschewed buns for the Double Down and also once saw fit to plunk a wad of pulled pork atop fried chicken sandwiches. Imagine all the things that old pirate captain, Silver, could shoot from his culinary cannon: perhaps some crazy Agent Orange spicy flavor? Maybe an exciting new shape, like that of a Jolly Roger flag or a blocked coronary? Why not TurDuckHen strips—the John Madden-approved Thanksgiving treat made miniature by embedding a chicken strip inside a duck strip inside a turkey strip?

Fingers were tingling with anticipation. Neck hair erect.

The chicken finally arrived. My denture-gnawing compadres and I began with a single strip. And it looked…like a Long John Silver's chicken strip. Ah, but it tasted…like a Long John Silver's chicken strip being eaten in a temp agency. No thermonuclear spices, no gamey hint of duck—nothing different than a usual stop at America's funniest-smelling restaurant chain. The computer quizzed me with an astounding 19 questions about this little white meat finger, such as:

MOISTNESS RANKING—Much too moist? Slightly Moist? Just Right? Slightly Too dry? Much too dry?

Followed by similarly structured questions regarding aroma, greasiness, color, breading thickness, juiciness, texture, aftertaste, and chicken flavor. That one, of course, begged the question: "So, wait, you can *adjust* the chickeniness?" With that, my appetite began to fade. Fingers no longer tingling. Neck hair disappointed.

Also, the computer quizzed us about saltiness. "Eh, not bad," I said.

Then another chicken strip arrived. And it tasted like…a Long John Silver's chicken strip. Nothing different from Bird One. Same roll call of questions. Lastly, came a third chicken strip, which tasted…yeah, you've figured this out by now. This taste test was less like a high seas culinary adventure and a lot more like comparing three different paint swatches of white. Each flavor was about the same and, with every successive bite, my tongue grew more swollen and numb—like pigging out on over-salted popcorn.

After a trio of strips, a sodium riot officially broke out in my mouth. Now my tongue was the one tingling. Neck hair, steady.

Next came a dual round of optional hushpuppies and another dozen questions, capped off with: "Is the onion flavor too strong, just right or not strong enough?"

The answer being: it doesn't matter.

We're talking about little fried dough balls rolled in salt. The elderly and I were tossing darts at opinion's wall. Same with the chicken. Sometimes a strip is just a strip. Relax, Long John.

Sitting there with a salt lick between my cheeks, I began wondering: what's the point of this taste test? Yes, the restaurant wants to dial in its flavors to perfection. But really, this is all a little desperate. We've become a society obsessed with revisionism.

We are all revisionists, constantly tweaking what is already good in the hopes of something *possibly* better. We can't settle for what we have, we can't leave well enough alone. It's what leads newspaper editors to look for someone possibly better than a music writer, when a rock critic would work just fine. It's all Coca-Cola's fault.

Back in 1985 the king of Soda Pop Mountain surprised everyone with New Coke. This is where the first revisionist stone rolled down the hill, swallowing up smaller bad ideas until it was boulder-sized and unstoppable. Someone in Atlanta said: "Hey, Coca-Cola's been the best-selling soft drink for a century, whaddya say we make it taste like Pepsi instead?"

Much like the sodium swamped birds I'd just packed away, New Coke's results were not good. But that mentality infected America until it spoiled my assistant editorial prospects and promises of free lunch.

After the test ended, writers and wrinklers were herded toward the exit. I was passed a crisp $20 bill in a white envelope like a classy hooker. It was sad. I vowed to win back my soul from Colonel Sanders and Admiral Silver.

How?

I was going to start settling. That's how.

There's a serious lack of settling in this world. We're all trying to be Coke, striving for some imaginary medal beyond the Gold.

Sometimes leaving well enough alone isn't such a terrible thing. It's hard, because there are more options for living, eating and entertaining than can possibly be dealt with. Hell, I can't go to the restroom without thinking about how my time could be optimized by sending a text, too.

I'm here to advocate simply leaving well enough alone. Do you have a fried length of chicken that already tastes pretty good? Super! Don't change a thing.

Are you dating someone who isn't a dream, but at least a few steps above a primate? Lock arms for life, my friend. Settle.

Me, I'm the poster child for settling.

Think about it: my mother and father could have been revisionists—seeking out the New Coke of kids. A better-looking son, a boy a few IQ points higher, or, at least, a child who can rate *chickeniness* without having a panic attack. Instead, they settled for me. Sure, my credentials will never land me a steady newspaper job, but I have Monday mornings open for free chicken and optional hushpuppies. I'd call that victory for settling.

THE WENTASTIC GUIDE TO FIREWORKS

And then there was the time a firecracker ate my fingers.

At least, that's what it felt like.

Let's call it the summer 1991. I was 11. I, like a lot of other misguided youths, thought biker shorts were a fashion statement. I also vaguely remember owning a Homey the Clown t-shirt. It was June, which meant I was working hard as an amateur pyrotechnician.

My parents, god love 'em, showed the questionable judgment of letting me play with firecrackers.

The Wensinks had just returned from a smuggling run across the border. Ohio has a lot of admirable qualities, but fireworks laws are not among them. The state doesn't sell anything more dangerous than sparklers and snakes. So, as a boy, we went to Indiana for our yearly Fourth of July display of fire breathing patriotism. This was a road trip, because Indiana was nearly two hours away. This illegal adventure was a staple of the summer season and pretty much the highlight of my young life each June.

You have to understand, I wasn't the kind of kid who had a sweetheart next door. I never even landed a serious girlfriend before I was 17. My first love was always fireworks.

Until that romance nearly cost some fingers.

We'd just returned from Indiana, car loaded with brightly colored explosives. It was dark out and my biker shorts and I were antsy. "Please, can I light one?"

"No." Mom said in the mist of the freezer. "We're having ice cream. Just eat a bowl and wait until the Fourth."

"Please, just one firecracker."

"No. It's dark."

"Exactly! They light up."

My mother caved. "Oh, fine. Just one."

We lived in the country, which meant no neighbors for a mile. No neighbors meant nobody was going to mind an early Fourth of July display. Everything was black and still, except for the sound of wheat in the wind, like sandpaper across wood.

As soon as my bare feet touched cold night grass, I ripped off the red wax paper like a Christmas gift. I couldn't untangle the braided wicks fast enough. These weren't life-ending M-80s or anything, just the standard birthday candle-sized crackers. I struck a bluetip match, held it to wick and tossed the featherweight explosive. Before it met the ground, the Black Cat went *Pow!* with a flash of orange in the darkness.

The crack echoed across miles of fields.

The satisfaction from this, I would eventually learn, was comparable to doing naughty things with the later loves of my life.

"Mom and dad might not have heard that one," I figured. "Just light another. Nobody will know." Thus, my childhood obsession was kicked into high gear. I was a gambler unable to walk away from the craps table.

I lit another, chucking it the minute my ears picked up the wick's sizzle.

Pow! Flash of orange. Shiver of joy.

This went on several times until I lit my final red beauty. But there was no slow sizzle of sparks. The wick went up like it was dipped in gasoline.

Mr. Biker Shorts didn't have time to react.

The sound exploded in my fingers, my ears were nothing but a ringing squeal and I violently shook that hand. A terror I'd never met flooded my body, standing in the dark, hopping up and down, whispering, "Oh-no, oh-no, oh-no, oh-no."

My fingers were numb. They were gone, I knew it.

With no thumb or forefinger I'd never play Nintendo again, I'd never shoot a basketball again, I'd never do naughty things with the later loves of my life. My fear was so huge that I couldn't force myself to look, knowing there'd be exposed blood and bone and not much else.

Still shaking the hand I ran into the house. "It blew up!" I screamed, flapping fingers like they were on fire.

My parents soothed me, showing me that all five digits were present. Not even a scorch mark. It was some sort of pyrotechnic miracle.

After a brief retirement I went back to my firecrackery ways, of course. Torturing Matchbox cars and GI Joes like some sort of Toys 'R' Us Dr. Mengele. There was still joy, but our love was fading.

And then—*Pow!*—20 years passed. In the amount of time it takes a bottle rocket to ignite, the summer fireworks season lost its charm. I filled that lust for Black Cats with video games and shooting hoops and miserably failing at doing naughty things with girls.

Before I knew it, I didn't think about fireworks. Before I knew it, I was 31 and it'd been decades since I lit a wick on anything more dangerous than pine scented candles.

That love was completely swept from my life.

But, recently, a fireworks catalog arrived in the mail. Addressed to me. Like a long-forgotten girlfriend sending a Facebook message.

Kentucky, too, is home to little more than sparklers. But Indiana, this time, was only a five minute car ride across the Ohio River. And, like an exploding Duty Free shop, the first exit off the highway had a fireworks emporium waiting for us less-fortunate Kentuckians.

Powder Keg Fireworks looked like it was housed in an abandoned supermarket. Because, well, it probably was. One month a year, it's Louisville's lifeline to all things sparkly and explosive. However, it must have another one-month gig, because there was a lot of garland and tinsel left along the top shelf of most racks.

No matter, because those racks were stocked for summer. This trip to Indiana as an adult was just as bomb-tastic as the ones as a boy. However, names like Saturn Rocket or Chinese New Year were antique titles like Packard and Hudson. Sepia-toned and quaint compared to modern explosives. Clearly, these new titles were workshopped by marketers, because they tried saying a lot about who purchases them.

A Guide to What Your Fireworks Say About You

Salute our Troops; Attack Iraq: This says: "I love this damn country and the freedom that comes with it." It also states: "I'm ready to accidentally burn down my neighbor's house to prove my point."

Mayan Temple; Sidney Harbor Bridge: This says: "I am a world traveler and a college professor. Watch me ignite this pyrotechnic display using only my pipe."

Purple Rain: This says: "There's only one way to come out of the closet on Uncle Sam's birthday and that's with a Prince-themed backyard barbecue."

Make it Rain: In an attempt to discourage amateur meteorologists, the manufacturers send a clear message, imprinting the paper walls of this brick with floating dollar bills. It says, "the next best thing to a stranger's vagina in your face is $45 worth of fireworks."

Absolute Pyro: (Featuring a non-flaming image of the capitol dome for whatever reason.) Saying: "I am Patriotic, but possibly illiterate."

Chicken on a Chain: Says: "I was in such a hurry to buy stuff, I didn't even read this one's label. Now, I'm worried my kids will think it's some weird sex-thing…Oh my god, is it?"

Gettin' It Done: Says: "I am going to skirt Larry the Cable Guy's copywritten slogan and deprive him of more sleeveless flannel shirts. Go America!"

One Bad Mother-in-Law: States: "Hmmmmm, Sarah's mom doesn't seem to get the hint when I mumble and slam beers in her presence. Perhaps this is the way to truly express my displeasure for my wife's maternal connection."

Butt Ugly Fountain; Dragon Farts: This says: "I got a fake ID and am using my allowance wisely." It also states: "I am a 31-year-old reliving a childhood fascination that nearly cost two fingers."

Walking the aisle, I realized two things. One, being the guy naming fireworks must be the best job in the world. Two, being the graphic designer for a fireworks company must require little more than being a seventh grader with limited Photoshop skills.

The elderly woman in charge of Powder Keg, with permed blonde hair and a chin waddle, found me in an aisle. "You comparing prices?" she said in a deep south accent. [**Wentastic Fact**: Residents of Southern Indiana tend to have much thicker accents than those just a few minutes away in Kentucky. Why? Beats me. Ask your local anthropologist.]

"Oh, uh," I stammered, hiding my little pad used to record all the awesome names. "No, I'm just taking notes…to tell my buddies about…so we can, you know, buy lots of fireworks." I got red as the sparks from a Dragon Fart.

"Uhh-huh…" she walked off, keeping an eye like I was a shoplifter or a sleeper cell.

Why did you lie? I thought. *Tell her you're a writer. Tell her about your forgotten love of fireworks. Mention almost losing your fingers once.*

It started haunting me, walking up the aisle of firecrackers— Black Cats stacked in packages as small as a bookmark and huge as a truck tire. Now, apparently, they also make something called Hydro-Crackers that explode underwater. Something the 1991 me would have given his right two fingers for.

But, 20 years later, I couldn't go through with it. I was filled with adult thoughts like, "My wife will be mad I wasted 15 bucks on firecrackers," and "Yikes, I bet this will make my tinnitus act up," and "is the perm lady watching? I should buy something to not look suspicious."

In the end, I walked away with two Dragon Farts and the comfort of retaining my fingers, as that firework does not explode.

I didn't realize it, but I did lose something when that Black Cat tried eating my fingers. No, not my fashion sense. (As everyone knows, biker shorts will never die!) Back in '91 I kept all my digits, thankfully, but lost that passion. Lost the invincibility of being young. And while the names are entertaining and the idea of fly-by-night fireworks shops is fascinating, that passion is something I'll never recapture.

I'm reminded of my one-time passion for shotgunning beers or my obsession with tracking down regional candy bars. In all those cases, it was good (for my liver and my teeth) that I lost that passion. But do we lose passion for good things, too? It makes me worry that stuff I'm passionate about now—writing, my wife, attempting to burn the house down making dinner—will also just become dusty nostalgia one day. And the scariest part, just like my love of fireworks, there's no way to know it's coming.

Worse, there's nothing I can do about it.

BORN FREE

There's a helicopter overhead. The blade spins with a sound-sucking *thwoop*. It dangles above you close enough to read the pilot's eye color.

Hundreds of children look up, praying for its cargo.

Thwoop-Thoop-Thwoop

This is the second time the black chopper has passed. High winds make it tough to steady itself. The brutal gusts also make you stuff your fingers into coat pockets. It's predictably cold this late in April, predictably for the Midwest.

Thwoop-Thoop-Thwoop

That lip-chapping wind is also why the precious cargo cannot be parachuted in. Beyond the blur of blades, the sky is dark and nasty—colored like bad dreams. The springtime aroma of wet newness is everywhere. Children wear shoes weighed heavy by mud, they jostle for position in a ragtag sort of line by the gate. The wire fence separates you and the drop zone. It's the barrier between chaos and calm. Luckily, they removed third base from the drop zone so nobody trips.

Thwoop-Thoop-Thwoop

And then something falls out the side of the midnight black copter. A Day-Glo pink parachute big enough for an action figure. The antsy kids go awestruck quiet, grumbling parents do likewise and you can't help but think, *That's it?*

Welcome to the Peep Drop 2011.

This is an annual tradition in Findlay, Ohio put on by a local religious organization. Every year they strap makeshift plastic parachutes to hundreds of boxes of Peeps. Peeps are, for the uninitiated, marshmallow globs shaped like baby chicks and dusted in pastel sugar. From there, the helicopter circles a local baseball diamond and drops the sweet dollops in a cavity-causing cacophony. Ideally, the sky is filled with Easter colors as they gently fall to the ground like a dream. Our young ones scurry in this fantasy-land mashup of Easter egg hunts and emergency military supply drops.

Thwoop-Thoop-Thwoop

All for free!

Thwoop-Thoop-Thwoop

The result is not quite the blizzard of happiness you imagine. Maybe your standards are too high, but the little Easter droplets leave the helicopter one at a time. Like a bunny making turds.

Eventually, a hundred or so peeps hit their mark, not counting the dozens that catch a gust and go sailing—likely to be discovered in the fields of surrounding counties by head scratching farmers. The kids rush out, grab a box and find their parents. The entire transaction lasts about 45 seconds.

But you'd waited around for over an hour at the indoor carnival beforehand. And you waited outside in the bone-humping cold for another half hour. All for a box of Peeps.

A box of Peeps costs roughly a buck, sometimes less. You can buy them anywhere from the gas station to the supermarket. And pretty much everyone who eats Peeps experiences a belly ache within minutes.

It would all be kind of a depressing way to celebrate a holiday if it wasn't for one thing: it is free.

Freebies carry the power of intoxication that would make Jack Daniel blush in his grave. What is it about free stuff that makes us so happy and so desperate to get in on the action?

Later that night, there is news of a fight breaking out at a Toledo gas station. Apparently, in an attempt to help recession-suffering drivers, a different church group doled out cards redeemable for free gasoline. At nearly $4 a gallon, this seems a little more important than sugar-coated faux poultry, but still, a fistfight?

That's what freedom does. It makes you woozy—it kicks your shins.

You, personally, can't help but hang onto that holey green shirt and duct tape-patched sleeping bag. You found them both in the FREE box at a yard sale in Oregon nearly five years ago. "I know they aren't in the best shape," you say to your wife, "but they were free." As if ridding yourself of these pickups would anger Cheapicus, the Greek God of coupons.

There was also that time (around the free sleeping bag and t-shirt era, incidentally) that you worked at a public defender's office for less money than what the neighbor boy makes mowing lawns. You had no interest in the law, nor any talent for administrative assisting, but the alternative was starvation. That poverty soon paid off in the form of stuffing your business card into restaurant fishbowls around town. The bowls were sponsored by a local investment firm, which proved to be just as desperate for money as you. They called a staggering four times, each saying: "Mr. Wensink, my name's Chip (or Sooz, or Skye or something equally naive) and I drew your card from our fishbowl at random. How about I treat you and some coworkers to lunch?" Lunch, shockingly, ranged everywhere from a pizza joint and a burrito place, to decent Indian fare and even a classy seafood restaurant. And every time you and your equally paycheck-to-paycheck coworkers showed up, the young financial advisor slumped his or her shoulders. "Oh, hello. *You're* Mr. Wensink? The one from the *law firm*?"

Little Cody or Becky or whoever probably had gold coins filtering through their eyes, thinking they'd get a crack at reorganizing some attorney's bank account. However, they learned lawyers weren't fishing for free meals, but the nonprofit defender's office and its staff of legal assistants were. The deal was: First, listen to their speech about how Scooter could help properly invest your money. Second, eat your free meal.

Dejected, these guys usually just wanted to get the hell out, saying something to the effect of: "You know, if any of you ever go to law school or something...um...here's my card. Investing is a smart idea...if, you know, you have money."

And then Tim and Dan and my other workmates dined for free. And it tasted good. Its freeness spiced the meal beyond normal pizza or tikka masala.

And then, with the *Thwoop-Thoop-Thwoop* disappearing off in the ugly, grey sky you see your nephew briefly in love with his baby blue parachuted Peeps. The look in the eyes says it all: another free stuff junkie has been born.

You never caught sugary snacks from a helicopter as a boy, but you still love to get something for nothing. Be it sample bread at the grocery, a concert at the park or someone's duct taped sex sack—freebies are rewarding. It's maybe the only sensation that doesn't dull over time. Well, that and crushing young financial advisors' dreams.

TED TURNER'S GONNA SHOOT
YER EYE OUT, KID

Right now, outside downtown Cleveland, a lamp is glowing. This lamp sits in the window of a modest two-story home. Heck, snow is probably falling as we speak. This lamp is shaped like a leg and covered in a fishnet stocking. This lamp is, most likely, the most famous lamp in cinema history. Somehow this sexy appendage has come to represent wholesome Christmas fun. This lamp belongs to the *A Christmas Story* House.

But I wonder, is Ted Turner trying to stuff this leg down my throat?

A Christmas Story is based on the comedic memoir by Jean Shepherd, and is a hazy warm tribute to Christmas, 1940. It follows the escapades of young, moon-faced Ralphie's attempts to convince his family he needs a BB gun from Santa. In between, tongues are frozen to flagpoles, the word "fudge" takes on a new meaning, and a host of other misfortunes fall upon Ralph and the rest of the Parker family.

A while back, I heard you could tour the Cleveland home where the film was shot. I'd been looking forward to seeing this holiday attraction since moving to nearby-ish Louisville. Finally, an opportunity arrived when I went to visit my old college buddies Ben, Don and Medved. I am drawn to this site much like little Ralphie was drawn to the power of a Red Rider BB gun. I have a sense of urgency, thinking, "I've got to check this out. The house is too weird to stay in business for very long. I mean, are there really more people than me who care enough about *A Christmas Story*? Enough to drive into one of America's fastest-dying cities, just to see a house from what should be considered, at best, a cult film?"

And so we track down this home in the scruffy Tremont neighborhood, just a few miles from downtown. People in Tremont don't have couches on their porches and cars on cement blocks in the yard. Not because the residents are economically above that. Hey, this is Cleveland. It's too cold 11 months out of the year to sit on the porch and who's going to clear all that snow from the yard to put the car up on blocks in the first place?

There are no signs off the road advertising *A Christmas Story* House. While all the neighboring homes are a little gray and sagging, the main attraction is the same mustard yellow with green trim made memorable in the film. And there is *the* lamp—that high-kicking, seductively glowing beacon—in the window. There is also a steep drop-off behind the home, leading to the Cuyahoga River (you may remember it as the body of water that caught fire once in the 60s) with a view of several factory smokestacks.

These elements fight my urge to enjoy the Christmas magic of this sacred spot, but I don't let it get me down. This is a special place. It's where the mastermind who directed *Porky's* and *Baby Geniuses* created one of the most treasured holiday films in history. You can keep Jimmy Stewart and *It's a Wonderful Life*, give me a bright lamp with a hint of ass cheek below the shade. Save Rudolph and his nuclear nose, give me a boy shooting his eye out with a BB gun. You can have Santa eating cookies and milk, I want Ralphie's mom stuffing a bar of Lifebuoy soap in his mouth.

The film was shot in 1983 and the house fell into disrepair until a few years ago when an investor from California bought the iconic home on eBay. Inexplicably, this gentleman turned it into a tourist attraction. Meanwhile, unbeknownst to me, Ted Turner— deep within his dark, stone castle in Atlanta—was brainwashing the planet.

A Christmas Story, as the tour guide points out, was a flop. Nobody paid to see it and the movie apparently gave critics polio. But, by some holiday gingerbread-scented miracle, I discovered it and fell in love. And apparently, according to the guide, so did 100,000 others who have made the pilgrimage to Cleveland.

"One-hundred thousand?" I think. "But I'm the only one who

loves this movie. It's my little secret. How is that possible? They were probably just lost and stopped for directions."

This question sits on the backburner as the tour begins. We enter the home and it looks just like the movie. There's a rough-looking Christmas tree, a BB gun hiding in the corner, oddly patterned wallpaper, a turkey waiting to be devoured by the Bumpus' hounds in the kitchen, Ralphie's bedroom and a Little Orphan Annie Decoder ring in the bathroom. Its time warp qualities are intoxicating. Some miracle of shrink-wrapping technology. Nothing has changed since 1983...except for the very sad-looking gentleman in a paperboy hat standing by the fireplace (more on him in a second).

"So, this is where they shot the bunny suit scene?" one woman asks as we mull around the living room, pointing to the stairs.

"Aw, that's where the mom broke the leg lamp," another says, admiring the living room window.

"Hey, is that the kitchen cabinet Randy hid in? '*Dad's gonna kill Ralphie.*'"

"No, actually," the guide says in a very rehearsed way. The way General Electric switchboard operators probably respond to the question of whether their refrigerators are running two-dozen times a day. "Most of *A Christmas Story* was actually shot on a soundstage in Toronto. The interior of the house didn't look like this at all. The crew actually only filmed a small portion of the exterior and the backyard sequences, like Black Bart's gang and Ralphie shooting his eye out."

Before this comment, there was a sweet helium in the air. A sparkly dash of wonderment. But now I can see something in everyone else's eyes: "We paid for a phony house? Let's just go upstairs, see the bedrooms and get back on the road."

Ben and Don and Medved and I diligently complete our tour, but kind of shrug things off. There's a little giggle about the bathroom actually having Lifebuoy and wondering where they got that soap— it hasn't existed for decades, right? In the backyard, with the view of some mammoth brown smokestack and the dense gray clouds, we peek into the shed that played such a big role in the movie. Give the House credit, it pays attention to a lot of detail, so we guess the shed will be filled with Black Bart's gang, eyes X-ed out. Instead, it looks like Jeffrey Dahmer's linen closet. At least five busted leg lamps in black fishnets are piled up, collecting dust and grit.

We go back inside for one final lap and notice something strange near the fireplace. That sad man, probably in his early 30s, wearing a paperboy hat and looking perpetually bored, is shaking someone's hand and giving an autograph.

"Who is that?" I ask the guide.

"Why that's Ian Petrella, he played Randy, Ralphie's kid brother who couldn't put his arms down in the snowsuit."

"Does he live here?"

"He lives in California, but comes back periodically to the house. He'll sign an autograph and tell you anything you want about the movie."

My mind can't crank out a single decent question, so we don't speak, Ian and I. It is all too much. I'm equally fascinated by all the hubbub and visitors one nearly-forgotten movie creates and also kind of depressed. We later learn that other bit players, like the grade school teacher and fur-hatted bully, Skut Farcas, return for holiday celebrations and (I'm not even making this up) *A Christmas Story* conventions.

All of these events and appearances and home renovations smell of money to be made. Money that Ted Turner, in his grinchiest Grinch costume, is counting from behind a barb-wired, gator-moated lair in Atlanta. I just didn't see it until the gift shop.

My friends and I decide to hit the gift shop because, well, it's here…we're here…what are we going to do, look at the smokestack some more? A neighboring home has been converted into a gift shop and I think it'll be a good time-waster. Probably a postcard of the famous house, a few copies of the movie, hey, maybe even a Red Rider BB gun!

Jeez Louise, was I wrong. This small bungalow is stuffed tight as a rich kid's stocking, but with *A Christmas Story* ephemera instead of Rolexes and gold bars (or whatever wealthy tykes get for Christmas). The place is floor-to-ceiling with junk that must have kept Chinese factories humming for months. We're talking adult and child-sized pink bunny suits, t-shirts with famous slogans (the aforementioned eye-shooting; "Oh, fudge"; "The pink nightmare"; "I triple-dog dare you"), blankets emblazoned with a cast photo, a Monopoly set, a checkers set, a Yahtzee! set, wrapping paper, paper cups, action figures, beer cozies, leg-lamp-shaped cookie molds, a Little Orphan Annie decoder ring and, no lie: bars of Lifebuoy Soap. The gift shop offers everything short of pre-frozen flag poles.

This isn't even counting the lamps. Leg lamps in four different sizes and wattages. From the genuine *fragilè*-sized to a desk lamp gam to sex-up your cubicle. You can even buy a replica of the famous wooden shipping crate the lamp arrived in.

At this point I need to clean my glasses and take a step back. "How the heck did all this get made? I thought I was the only one who watched *A Christmas Story*?" I think. But clearly, though I don't currently see anyone purchasing these goods, someone saw fit to produce this stuff. People must buy it, right?

It hits me that during those 24-hour marathons TBS runs every year, I'm probably not the only one watching. Okay, that makes sense. But still, it was an important part of growing up. Is it actually possible it was for everyone else's childhood, too? Then Ben and Don and Medved and I begin talking. The more we think about it, *A Christmas Story wasn't* part of our childhoods. We'd never heard of it until about 1998, about the time those all-day feedings of the movie were crammed down our mouths like pink bars of soap.

I finally realize one man was doing the cramming. Right here, amongst a marketing blitz I haven't seen since the 1980s *Star Wars* heyday, I piece everything together. The back of my ticket claims, in cataract-inducing print, that *A Christmas Story's* copyright is held by the Turner Broadcasting Company. Ted Turner's pride and joy.

For those uninitiated in their Georgia television mogul history, Turner owns Turner Classic Movies, CNN, TNT and…of course… TBS: Home of the day-long celebration of all things Ralphie. There it is, but like the mom in the movie and that lamp, I don't want to look at it. If I ignore the facts, maybe my happy memories will eventually crawl back home. I don't want to see that my nostalgia and the special feeling of being the only person on Earth who loves *A Christmas Story* has been somehow orchestrated.

Did Turner simply wave his basic cable wand and create a cult film?

Yes, I'm starting to think that's exactly what Ted's team of marketers/scientists/Chinese factory workers and astronauts (oh, Turner has astronauts, don't kid yourself) have done. A little bit of research shows that Turner took over the rights to the movie after purchasing MGM pictures and that the 24-hour marathon quietly made its debut in 1997. Right around the time these nostalgic memories embedded themselves.

Does this make the movie somehow tainted? Of course not. *A Christmas Story* is still fun. I will be quoting that baby until I die. (Personal favorite: "Whoopee, a zeppelin!") In fact, the movie's message is perfect for this entire Turner-ized fiasco in Cleveland. The heart of *A Christmas Story* is about disappointment and coping with that disappointment, no matter how brutal.

A Christmas Story basically says: Hey, your parents don't want you to have a BB gun? Teacher doesn't want you to have it? Hell, Santa doesn't even want you to be armed? On top of that, bullies are punching your lights out? Dogs ate your Christmas dinner? You actually *did* shoot your eye out? The movie simply says: Oh, well, keep plugging along. Good things'll happen.

And that helps my holiday glee return, if only a little more ragged than I remember.

It just makes you wonder, if Turner's brainwashing succeeds, what next? Will we soon see quick cash-in attractions that let you take a ride in Bill Murray's limo from *Scrooged*, visit the *Ernest Saves Christmas* house, purchase replicas of Sinbad's mailman costume from *Jingle All the Way*?

Let's just say I'll spot you *A Christmas Story*, Ted Turner. That makes me feel good, even when times are sucky. But the minute I start seeing the 48-hour *Fred Claus* marathon, it'll take an army of Red Rider BB guns to keep me from storming your Atlanta castle.

BLACK CHRISTMAS

Grandma loved Russian roulette underneath the mistletoe. It was a holiday tradition. Up until her fifth husband, Ed, won.

And then there was the way we'd always sing "Hark the Herald Angel" in the parking lot when daddy got out of jail each Christmas Eve. Except when he didn't display necessary good behavior.

Ah, but let's not forget that December 25 I spent in the ICU after trying to shimmy down the chimney of the orphanage to deliver puppies to all those sad kids…

Okay, wait, none of that ever happened.

I don't actually have any insightful holiday stories of depression and redemption. Or even tales of dramatic dark-meat-induced family fisticuffs. Like a lot of other Santa Claus celebrants, my holiday usually isn't all that noteworthy. The Wensinks get along pretty well and burglars never once attempted daring nighttime Teddy Ruxpin heists.

So, in lieu of personal drama, I will focus on the holiday heartbreak of others. Namely, Frank Sinatra. Specifically, Sinatra's 1957 non-classic album, *A Jolly Christmas*.

Not that you asked, but it's my vote for best holiday album of all time.

But be warned, *A Jolly Christmas* is a yuletide horse tranquilizer of a record. And this is coming from me, a guy who genuinely enjoys Christmas music.

Its dozen tracks are each familiar holiday classics, but something is off on every cut. That something is Sinatra.

From the bottom of history's bobsled run, 1957 looks like a

stocking-load of awesomeness for Saint Frank. Flipping through the man's catalog, one would imagine *A Jolly Christmas'* tunes would belt from speakers with the gusto of Sinatra's JFK/mafia poker nights. In the last half of the 50s, Frankie's Midas Touch was going atomic. A quick check of the All Music Guide shows 3-star *Jolly Christmas* bumpered by a handful of 5-star, solid-gold up-tempo classics, including *Songs for Young Lovers, A Swingin' Affair!* and *Come Fly With Me.*

With 1957-era Francis Albert, too, one would expect the Playboy Mansion version of our favorite carols. Here was a man dressed in a tailored suit with beautiful women flapping toward him like sparrows in *The Birds.*

Yes, in '57 everything was perfect for Frank.

Except, he was probably looking for a gun barrel to swallow. Old Blue Eyes was choking down a chicken bone of misery while recording an ode to the hap-hap-happiest season of all. No big deal.

A little research shows *A Jolly Christmas* isn't Frankie's ironic addition to December's tower of glee. It is, likely, a direct reflection of a man who once referred to himself as: "An eighteen-karat manic depressive." The same fella Gay Talese said could easily plunge "into a state of anguish, deep depression, panic, even rage."

A Jolly Christmas is *that* guy singing.

The album pries apart Sinatra's cool and further illuminates this Zoloft-gulping profile, subtly revealing the distant, difficult Sinatra in Talese's famous *Esquire* piece, "Frank Sinatra Has a Cold."

The cause of ol' Velvet Vocals' anguish: genuine heartbreak. And, probably, a case of reverse Seasonal Affective Disorder.

Love kicked Sinatra in the teeth twice in 1957. First, from divorcing his wife of six years, Ava Gardner. Second, he quickly fell in love with Lauren Bacall only to end up embarrassed by a very public and ill-timed marriage proposal.

Slap those rough patches atop the fact that Casanova was stuck singing about The Little Town of Bethlehem and sleigh rides during June and July and you've got a recipe for something grim. On June 14, for example, Los Angeles temperatures peaked at 104-degrees. A thermostat mark that still stands. Not exactly blizzardly inspiration. Mixing the delicate miseries of heartbreak and poor timing into the fruit cake that is *A Jolly Christmas* all adds up to

Sinatra's vocal wrist-slicing.

And it's wonderful to witness.

"Somber" is how I'd describe the album today. If you and I were sitting under the doug fir in my living room, splitting a bottle of scotch, I'd tell you how this is the only record that depicts real holidays: depressing and made worse by pretending to enjoy the company of relatives. Not to mention all the claymation.

"Lazy" is how I would have described that same album a few years ago if you and I were under the same tree with a bottle. (Jeez, we might have a drinking problem.)

A Jolly Christmas is one of those tricky 100-level philosophy finals where *all* the answers are correct. It's both lazy and somber, but without a doubt the finest holiday album ever recorded. Yes, Sinatra clearly phoned it in for this studio session. But the results are all the better for Captain Fedora's total disregard for listener enjoyment.

When I purchased *Jolly Christmas* in Everyday Music's dollar bin five years ago, I expected a jazzy, hipster Ratpack holiday romp for an upcoming Christmas party. What I got, instead, was a lone stab at swingtime swagger ("Jingle Bells") that utilized a scat-singing choir to pull a *Weekend at Bernie's* number on the song. The Chairman of the Board had been dragged at gunpoint into the booth. Thankfully, "Jingle Bells" is the perfect setup for the 11 dark Christmas carols that follow.

To say Sinatra isn't trying very hard on this album is like making some joke about the French army. It wouldn't be surprising to learn the orchestral director needed to check Frank for a pulse at points. And Frankie Sin's adrift ambition doesn't even blip on the same radar of charm that made Dean Martin's so-drunk-I-forgot-the-lyrics-to-"Frosty the Snowman" routine such a favorite around our house. My early assessment of *Jolly Christmas* was that Old Blue Eyes was simply cashing a check, probably buying his latest lover a snow leopard or a moon rock or a computer the size of Rhode Island—whatever rich folks did back then.

And that remained my opinion for several years until one tree decorating session opened my eyes. White lights cast a dim glow and my liver burned bright with my usual decorating bourbon, which helped me understand *Jolly Christmas* isn't a lazy album, it's a purposefully depressing album. The record is a beautifully emotive suicide note to holiday discomfort that other artists don't have the balls to release.

From the plucked strings of "Mistletoe and Holly," to the naked "Silent Night" to a reindeer-jerky-gnawing version of "Have Yourself a Merry Little Christmas," this is a record not fit for family dinners and giftwrap, but for TV dinners and lonesome sobbing.

Sinatra bellows all the familiar tunes fans demand, but through a clenched jaw. It's not unlike getting stuck talking to your weird uncle, Salvatore, listening to him discuss the finer points of parakeet breeding for an hour before the turkey is carved. And like that holiday unhappiness, not far beneath a gloss of comfort and familiarity lurks a dark pool that can only be reflected by the album's cover.

Black.

Probably the only Christmas album this side of *Holiday Greetings from Glenn Danzig* to wear so much negativity on its sleeve. The darkness of the painted picture of Sinatra on the cover is a perfect reflection of the icy etching within the record grooves. Which is what makes *A Jolly Christmas* absolutely essential.

Voyeurism is the best medicine. That's true with Sinatra's *A Jolly Christmas*. The record shows how your life can be so much more painful and tragic, even though this world's already full of enough pain and tragedy as it is. Though it requires a stiff drink as accompaniment, *A Jolly Christmas* makes you want to embrace family that much closer. Even Uncle Sal and his tales of parakeet woe.

HANGING UP THE HORNS

Since the pioneers founded Reno, NV, couples have filed divorce papers for a blizzard of reasons. Just ask somebody who's done it a few times, like most of Hollywood, or millionaires, or someone with an addiction to rented formal wear.

But has anyone ever been divorced for impersonating a bull?

It seems I might be just the husband to test this theory.

It starts, like so many of the high-water marks of life, with drinking.

"Is *The Bull* coming out tonight?" I hear people ask probably once per social gathering.

"We want The Bull! We Want The Bull!"

"Come on, please."

Parties, family holidays, dental appointments, you name it. This question finds my ears over and over again like a tipsy buddy who forgets for the fifth time that he already told you about his sweet new apartment. It's *Groundhogs Day*, but with bourbon and imitation cattle.

"You'll have to ask Leah," I say, usually chain-guzzling whiskey to help fight the bullish urge. My hands start to shake, aching to form horns. But, like a gentleman, I direct my fans to my wife.

Her answer, as always, is, "Hell, no."

And then I have to watch their smiles sink into disappointment. I have to pretend I don't see the boozy glimmer in their eyes, thinking: *He's putting us on. The Bull has to come out.*

It's hard letting people down like this.

The Bull, sadly, has hung up his horns in the name of marital bliss. But that doesn't mean he doesn't want to strut out into that intoxicated bullring one more time.

The Bull, you see, is a party trick I do.

Or, rather, a party persona I step into when my mood and blood alcohol level are just right.

Don't get your hopes up, there's nothing overly amazing about The Bull. At least from my hazy memories of Bulldom. The maneuver was born years ago, the night before my brother-in-law, Will's, wedding. Our group went out for drinks, ending up at some empty townie bar within walking distance of my house. For reasons still unclear, we requested lemon drop shots and tequila. The bartender could pour tequila no sweat, but admitted the best he could do on the shot was vodka and lemon juice.

They were both bottom shelf and disgusting.

Undaunted, we drank at least five each. Then a piece of liquor-time *magic* stampeded into my life.

Bos Taurus. Texas Longhorn. Angry steak. Now known simply as: The Bull.

Walking home at closing time, I stuck out both index fingers from my fists, situated them atop my skull and started charging at the rest of my wobbly group. I said I was trying to "gore" them. "Beware! *I am The Bull!*"

Eventually, imaginary red capes were waved before me. I stamped and snorted and usually tackled that unfortunate matador into a neighbor's grass. I recall lots of laughter and others lining up for a piece of the action. I was a black angus Stallone taking on all arm wrestlers in *Over the Top*.

Inspired by blurred vision, I brought out The Bull a few more times after that. The inebriated duel between man and beast was always a hit.

Now, whenever my speech starts slurring, I hear cries of "Toro! Toro!" from various friends and relatives and law enforcement officers around the Louisville Metropolitan area.

But, sadly, The Bull remains penned. I have a distinct feeling if I brought our four-legged friend out of retirement, I'd end up before a judge with my wife on her own separate side of the aisle.

Leah hates The Bull.

It annoys her. It scares her. It causes the two of us to fight.

She is a much more articulate arguer when drinking, which means I usually lose these fights. Which means I hate these battles all the more.

Why all the fuss, right?

As best I can recall, I don't attempt to gore her. I never leave hoof prints in the carpet. Not once have I shat in the kitchen. Never! But, still, when a party crowd starts howling for the horns she shoots a look that says: "Absolutely not!"

"I don't know why," she tells me tonight when I ask why she hates The Bull so much. "It's embarrassing."

"I won't tackle you."

"I just don't want to have to take the bull home, is all."

"But people love The Bull!"

"I think everyone likes it because they like seeing you make a fool of yourself."

And like that—whispering in the kitchen so our newborn (Daddy's little veal) doesn't wake from all the bullshit—my feelings are hurt.

That sinking in my chest isn't because Leah hates The Bull. Her vegan leanings for party entertainment are an established fact. I'm okay with that. Just like she knows I get annoyed when I have to spend more than 20 minutes at IKEA, she also accommodates. It's called "compromise," bachelors, look it up.

These damaged feelings come from the likelihood that my friends and family are laughing *at* me. Am I this popular because it helps them feel better, thanking God they're not as drunk or as clumsy as this side of beef?

It's confusing.

It reminds me of hearing through the childhood grapevine that the guys you thought were your friends call you "nerd" and do impressions of you behind your back. It's like a girlfriend dumping you with little more than a shrug of the shoulders. It's not unlike a cop just smirking when you say you don't know the answer to: "Do you know why I pulled you over today?"

The confusion and sadness help me make a difficult decision. The Bull will stay retired.

The point being, sacrifices must be made in life. Sometimes you have to let down an entire room full of people in order to make one person happy. Sometimes our bovine needs simply cannot be met whether you are the Bull or the Matador. It'll be hard saying goodbye to my beefy alter ego. Hopefully he'll go more gracefully out of this world than he stampeded into it.

FALLOUT, OH-BOY

You are now under Wendy's.

You are now under K-Mart.

You are now in a hole. A mega-hole. Louisville's MEGAcavern, to be exact. And you are about to reconsider everything you ever thought about nuclear war and earthworms.

The Wensinks are a cave-crazy bunch. We're practically Cro-Magnon, we love cave dwelling so much. Childhood vacations were little more than one guided cave tour after another before reaching the beach. If we saw a sign for CAVE TOURS we were attracted like sunburns to Irish skin. You name it: Morengo Cave, Old Man's Cave, Mammoth Cave, Nick Cave and the Bad Seeds—we saw them all over the course of 18-or-so summer vacations. My older sister, for reasons still unknown, was the main cave-junkie. Things couldn't get stalactite-y enough for her. I've squeezed through claustrophobic crevasses, admired ancient wall doodles, even ridden a boat across an underground lake inhabited by eyeless fish.

No lie. Blind-ass fish.

I'd been looking forward to reliving my childhood and touring the MEGAcavern since moving to Louisville. What's not to love? It's a cave that supposedly stretches all the way underneath the city, probably full of beautiful rock formations, autumn-cool temperatures and geological razzmatazz.

It wasn't long after I buckled into my seat that I began questioning why I was so excited. Why were the Wensinks ever excited about caves? What about all those other visitors? What was their big infatuation?

Our country is covered with these attractions. Wherever man discovered a giant gap on his property, he charged admission and made it into an attraction. One guy in Portland literally dug a 10-foot hole in his backyard and called it "The Woodstock Mystery Hole." They're everywhere, but why? What's our fascination with the dark, scary places?

Down in the MEGAcavern things hadn't even gotten dark and scary yet. Little did I know those creepy eyeless fish would seem like the Care Bears once I clawed my way out of the cavern. No easy feat, since this sucker features 90-foot solid-rock ceilings, 17 miles of tunnels, massive rock pillars the size of bungalows and is rumored to be large enough to fit two Empire State buildings. I figured it'd be like touring an airplane hanger made of stone—a natural miracle or the Eighth Wonder of the World hiding directly below the Louisville Zoo.

But then I met Stephen.

Shortly thereafter, the nightmares began.

Stephen was our thick-waisted, jolly-faced tour guide. Ol' Steve gave us a little background that instantly brought me down to Earth. "MEGAcavern was once the largest limestone mine in the state of Kentucky," he said into a Fisher-Price-quality microphone. This meant that, no, I wasn't preparing to enter a mind-boggling feat of natural erosion and stalagmite ingenuity. Rather, some hole carved out by jackhammers and dynamite.

But this wasn't the stuff of nightmares yet. Just the stuff of mild disappointment. I'm okay with that, my whole life has been a series of mild disappointments. We're like old roommates. Disappointment and I go way back.

"Have no fear," Stephen said, starting up the Jeep that towed our wagon. "There is nothing down here that can jump out of the dark and hurt you. No animals. No birds. Nothing."

Fair enough, Steve, but being mauled hadn't crossed my mind… until you mentioned it. Probably not the best introduction. Stephen peppered his delivery with little uncomfortable "Ahhhs" and "ummmms" slipping out at inappropriate moments.

"Also," he said, "You do not have to worry about rockslides, collapses or cave-ins." Again, something that hadn't really bothered me…until *now.*

Stephen rambled off the many benefits of limestone's strength. "We are so deep underground we wouldn't even feel a nuclear bomb strike!"

Good God, Steve, is it your first day? Is that the best example you could think of? Especially, when you're trying to *ease* people's fears.

Oh, but Steve was a human medicine cabinet full of anxiety pills like this. "Again, there is no risk of danger down here...ah, um...but just in case, I'm required to point out that there are exits carved into the rocks every three-hundred feet. These will lead you to ground level...but you won't need them. Perfectly safe down here.

"Actually, the biggest danger down here is my Jeep catching on fire. But that won't happen and if it did, there's an extinguishing system onboard, just like NASCAR uses."

Again, Steve, not something I was worried about, but now that you mention it, we are awfully close to your pipe bomb on wheels.

"But," Steve said as I developed a neck cringe whenever he said that word. "Ah, hypothetically speaking, if there *was* a fire, like a big fire, we took the liberty of installing that fireproof hallway you see to your right." He pointed to a long black box big enough to stand in. "It's pressurized and can withstand any blaze for up to two hours. We'd be perfectly comfortable during a fire...but there is no risk of fire."

So, let's get this straight. No risk of injury or fire, but the proprietors of this hole in the ground decided to spend thousands of dollars just for kicks? And, wait a second, *caves* can catch on *fire*? When did this happen? Let me guess, there's no danger of a grizzly attack, but just in case you've laid out bear traps every 50 yards.

"Also." Here was another part of Stephen's vocabulary that meant instant ulcers. "There are radio outlets throughout the cave, so the fire department can stay in contact with its headquarters. That is... ah, if there needed to be a fire department down here. But there won't. Perfectly safe." He ground the Jeep into gear and we were off.

Now that every dew drop landing on my shoulder gave me a heart attack, we were on the move. "Finally," I figured. "We'll learn about rocks and mining and this trip won't be so bad. Educational. Nostalgic." I remembered, as a little runt, playing Indiana Jones, running around Old Man's Cave, having the time of my life.

But education, apparently, was not on the top of MEGAcavern's list. The next 10 minutes consisted of some JC Penney-rejected mannequins wearing bib overalls meant to resemble miners. Stephen's commentary went something like, "limestone…*mumble mumble*… mining, ah-um, dynamite…*mumble mumble*…money. Stopped mining in 1970s…ah, I don't know why they stopped."

Everywhere we went, little metal signs told us how far we'd traveled. We're under the Wendy's. We're under K-Mart. We're under the University.

Stephen's voice perked up and my neck twitch didn't like it one bit. "Did you know," the suddenly peppy guide said. "This was the biggest fallout shelter in America during the cold war? That's right. It was outfitted to house fifty-thousand of Kentucky's most important politicians, doctors, policemen and Fort Knox soldiers in case of a nuclear attack. But if you weren't on that list, you were on your own, *up there*."

"Jeez, Stephen," I thought. "That's about as comforting as your little safety speech earlier."

Oh, but Mr. Happy-go-Lucky wasn't done yet.

"You'll notice this concrete wall here." I had, it was a massive slab, taller than my home. "Unlike the natural limestone pillars carved out by mining, the, ah, city inspector made us construct this. Um, we were told to build this to prevent collapses. Ah…but there will be no collapses. Nothing to worry about." And then, shifting gears, like cocktail party small talk: "Now, let me show you an informative film on this cement wall all about nuclear attacks."

Wait, what? I don't remember atomic bombs being a discussion point at Morengo Cave when I was a boy.

For the next five minutes we were treated to some film the MEGAcavern dug out of a public school closet. Stephen used this fishy cement wall as a projector's screen. It was one of those informative film strips that would be kitch and fun if the subject wasn't about how nuclear war was *pretty much* inevitable. The scratchy film stock informed us that even if the Bomb doesn't hit our city, the fallout will blanket America and reward us with a slow, disfigured, cancer-tastic death.

Stephen, here's a tip: Probably not a great idea to show a film about death and Armageddon on a wall that may or may-not prevent a cave-in. Kind of makes us anxious.

Just a tad.

But they didn't do anything small here. It's not called the Tad-O-cavern and there's a reason.

After a few minutes of pitch blackness we were whisked off to a magic rocky corner that took the creepiness many, many…uh, many tads further than the film.

"This is an actual recreation of a fallout shelter in operation," he announced before taking us for a lap around a football field-sized camp of nuclear depression. Here, the JC Penney mannequin rejects numbered in the hundreds and were lying in puddles of water, leaning over card tables and standing above make-believe bonfires. One nude statue, with his lower half obscured by wooden planks, took a shower in overhead drippage. These lucky nuclear attack survivors all wore moth-eaten, disintegrating clothes. Their wigs were matted with water. Worst of all, their glassy, wooden faces were lit by harsh footlights, making each pitiful "survivor" look like that guy from the Halloween movies having a sad day.

This scene, signifying those special men and women lucky enough to survive World War III, made me glad I wasn't a politician, doctor, policeman or soldier. I was suddenly relieved that if something catastrophic ever happened, guys like me probably aren't high on the government's "Dudes to Rescue" list. Suddenly, an eyeball-less fish lake sounded like the Hilton.

In between horrifically staring down one mannequin who I *swore* was watching me, I asked that initial question again. What is the draw of caves and caverns? Why pay good money to hang out in the darkest, dampest spots on Earth? This didn't even touch upon the Eiffel Tower of all questions: "If you are a cavern owner and lucky enough to entice paying customers into your dank, ugly hole, why scare the crap out of them and make them eager to die?"

"Did you know there was one person on the list of fifty-thousand that wasn't a politician, a doctor, a policeman or soldier?" the sunshine and rainbows guide said. "Can you guess who it was?"

Our little crowd was silent. Probably like me, first wondering what the hell they'd gotten into and secondly, looking frantically for the nearest *just-in-case* EXIT door.

"It was Kentucky Fried Chicken's own Colonel Harlan Sanders," he said with a Sesame Street tone. "Because, you can't have nuclear holocaust without the eleven secret herbs and spices."

Silence. Deep, cave silence. We came down here for many reasons, but Armageddon comedy was not one of them.

Stevie Boy cleared his throat. "On to the next part of our tour, the *worm farm!*"

At this point my defenses were chipped down to nothing. After visiting what I thought would be one of nature's wonders only to discover a limestone hole and the post-apocalypse Penney's display from Hell, the only response was, "Sure. Of course. Why not a worm farm?"

The fabulous worm farm, our tour group learned through exhausted, kill-me-please eyes, was a pine box about the shape of a fat man's casket. Stephen informed us this was green recycling in action because the box was full of paper. He claimed worms eat paper like frat boys consume chicken wings: quickly and with frequent trips to the bathroom. Their worm waste-filled dirt is then sold as fertilizer.

"And," Stephen said with a Christmas morning grin. "Worms are high in protein. Eighty-percent protein and very healthy."

Frankly, I suspected everyone else saw this coming, too. But the tour group was powerless at that point. It would have been like spitting to diffuse a stick of dynamite.

"So healthy in fact..." Stephen's thick fingers began rummaging around the worm farm the way I look for the last unbroken pretzel in a bag.

"Please, Stephen," we all thought. "Is this necessary? Just take us back to the gift shop. Back to daylight."

"...you can eat 'em." And Captain Cave Man lifted out a squirmy long worm, dusted off the valuable fertilizer and swallowed the fish bait like a happy carp.

So, just to keep score, at this point our tour group **1.)** Felt robbed of $13 for this tour; **2.)** Feared for its life because this cavern is obviously oh-so-safe and fireproof [Did I mention there was NO risk of animal attacks?]; **3.)** Was looking forward to death instead of being saved from a nuclear strike; and **4.)** Was ready to vomit.

This was, thankfully, the grand finale. Sure, we passed Kentucky's largest underground boat and RV storage facility. (Is there more than one?) Part of the "underground business park" the MEGA-cavern also houses in order to make ends meet during America's economic roller coaster ride.

The big question was still lingering in my mind as we neared the exit: why do entrepreneurs open the doors on these things in the first place?

That seemed easy after we learned the local Hershey's distributor keeps all its stock down in this pit-'o-sadness because the chocolate will neither melt nor freeze at this temperature. It's a uniquely human point of view that everything can be used for moneymaking. We're told from the time our umbilical cord is snipped that you and you and even *you*, cheerful Stephen, can be a millionaire or a president or on one of those ballroom dancing reality shows. All you have to do is use your noggin and riches are only a dream or two away. No matter how ill-advised the venture.

Where the pessimist sees one of the world's largest underground holes, the optimist envisions life differently. Glass half-fullers acquire a massive, dormant limestone mine and say, "Imagine the *possibilities*! What can we do here?"

The answer, obviously, is fill visitors with so much anxiety they are actually thankful they'll die instead of spending the rest of their life in a cave, eating worms cooked in the Colonel's eleven secret herbs and spices.

Walking down a long hallway toward natural light, I hate it, but I see a little of myself in Stephen. Not so much the uncomfortable bug eating, but um-ing and ahhhh-ing your way through your 20s. I'll bet a hundred mannequin heads our guide had no intention of eating worms for a living, but it's all there was. He, too, probably wondered why MEGAcavern was in business, like I did.

Clearly, what repulsed me most of all in this den-'o-depression was how much I saw my own desperation in Stephen and this empty space.

TWO BONGS DON'T MAKE A RIGHT

If you know me, you know I am no stranger to the dark corners of juvenile delinquency. You might remember the national headlines from 1997: TEEN ARRESTED FOR LOITERING.

No?

Jeez, do you pay much rent living under that rock? Okay, I'll refresh your memory. 17-year-old Patrick was hanging around the parking lot of his hometown's only pizza parlor on a Friday evening, talking to friends—neither causing a ruckus, drinking beer (big brothers and fake IDs were a thin commodity in 1997) or having a backseat wrestling match with a cheerleader (you'll also recall that in 1997, boys who neither caused a ruckus or scored beer got laid).

This was back when the internet was little more than a sonogram photo of the wild child it would quickly become, cell phones were for Zach Morris and TiVo was the name of that foreign exchange student who smelled funny. I lived in a small town and had no choice but to take pleasure in particularly Amish delights like standing and chatting with other humans.

Not exactly public enemy-type activity. But, my village's sole policeman didn't agree.

It must have been a slow night because he screeched into the parking lot with flashers strobing red and blue. Young Pat was charged with loitering.

This previous brush with the wrong side of the law recently came back to my foreground. My wife and I ran into America's new generation of juvenile shenanigans. The only loitering, however, was done by a leafy green plant.

If you guessed the neighbor boy (also 17) decided he'd try growing marijuana on our garage roof, you get the golden pot leaf for the day.

Okay, stop right there, smart-ass.

I realize I'm no longer 17 and a little out of touch with what young bucks do for entertainment. I couldn't name a Lady Gaga tune if it was tattooed on my wife's arm. The internet is getting harder and harder for me to understand. Plus, I actually found hair growing out of my ears the other day. But it's difficult not to think we're going to be doomed because today's juvenile delinquents are remarkably dumber.

Remember, this is coming from a guy who was arrested for *standing*. I know a thing or two about dumb crime.

The fifth of July was a sweet one this year because Uncle Sam's birthday fell on a Sunday, meaning there was no work Monday. Like any red, white and blue blooded American, I called my mommy that day. Midway through our chat I told Mamma W I had to let her go, something looked weird was atop the garage.

Keep in mind, our one-car garage is in the back yard, has a flat roof and is no more than eight feet tall. So it's pretty obvious when there's a large green flower pot atop it. A flower pot we didn't own.

My wife and I had been cautioned by a neighbor weeks earlier that the boy a few doors down had been getting into back yards and acting suspicious. This fella had dropped out of school and was unemployed, which apparently left a lot of free time to roam the wide open spaces of Louisville.

Spaces including our garage roof.

While not the greatest student or job-holder, this criminal genius must be an excellent horticulturist. When we dug out the ladder and climbed the roof, we discovered this wasn't a bouquet of daisies—delivered to our roof by some FTD snafu—but, instead, something resembling Bob Marley's garden.

Inside our little gift pot was, well, the gift of pot. I've never grown weed, but have seen enough Grateful Dead tapestries and Snoop Dogg albums to get an idea of what we're dealing with.

Frankly, I am a little jealous of our neighborhood Wavy Gravy. This kid's raising hearty crops and, meanwhile, I can't grow cherry tomatoes to save my life.

I'm sure a lot of people would have yipped for joy and started cycling through brownie recipes before getting this little bundle down from the garage. But we decided to be good, square citizens and phone the authorities.

"Really?" was all we could say. "On what planet does he think someone fails to notice a grow-op atop their garage?"

Back in 1997—when I was loitering like a statue—we heard about this kind of stuff. Guys with fluorescent lights and hydroponic greenhouses in their closet. Secret clearings in the woods supposedly flush with smokable gold. But a neighbor's roof? Come on, even the loitering version of Al Capone knew better.

I try to be an open-minded dude. If you want to grow weed, knock yourself out. Times are tough, we all need to get creative with money-making. But, me, I have my hands full with a rotting crop of cherry tomatoes, so I don't really want my garage being used to rub my nose in someone else's agricultural success.

I'm not upset about the drugs. The neighbor could have just as easily been hiding stolen diamonds in that flower pot and I'd be equally disturbed. It's insulting to assume I'm so dumb or out of touch that I don't know what's going on atop my own garage.

Our confusion just kept repeating as our jaws dropped a little further. "Really, man? You're just going to hop on our roof and grow pot? Maybe you'd like to use our cats as heroin mules? Or raise magic mushrooms in my cupboards.

Mi casa es su casa. Go nuts.

A portly, good-humored police officer soon arrived, climbed the ladder and informed us: "Well, it sure looks like marijuana. But, of course, we can't be sure until we smoke it."

Instead of finding his bong and digging out a Phish album, the officer proceeded to call about six other cops and drug detectives to my yard. A quick tour of the back alley revealed two similar growing operations in an elderly neighbor's yard. Our street suddenly turned into Little Jamaica.

Eventually, two detectives moseyed over to the boy's house for what they called, "a knock-and-talk." Johnny Appleseed, unfortunately, wasn't home. I'm sure he was reading Chaucer to senior citizens or, at the very least, studying for the SAT.

The police did, however, take a little tour and uncovered (big shock) a small cash crop also growing in his bedroom. Apparently, my garage was this kid's overstock department.

At that point, the cops stopped updating us with the investigation. My assumption is that things aren't going to go too well for Beaver Cleaver. My first reaction was "good riddance" and I hope this kid gets in some serious trouble for dragging me into this mess.

But then I felt guilty. No matter how misguided his world already is, I might have inadvertently screwed it even further. I hope not. I'm a big believer in redemption and this kid's life is far from over, considering the juvenile slap on the wrist he'll likely get. But I'm a little worried, not only for this doofus, but all the other boneheaded teenagers, too.

Ideally, this teen will soon grow up and probably get a job. And I hope he makes something good happen. Given his low IQ and propensity for narcotics, he's already on the fast-track to holding public office. [**WENTASTIC FACT:** many politicians got their start as criminals. Herbert Hoover was a notorious horse thief, John Quincy Adams paid for college as a male prostitute and Abe Lincoln built the world's first meth lab in a one-room log cabin.] But even if he's fixing plumbing or replacing brake pads in the future, those are important jobs. Jobs I don't want a complete moron handling. So, I have got some gnawing worries about the nation's weak criminal element. Smart kids tend to land on their feet in some manner of speaking. But our country is already spinning down the drain. How will it be when it's run by guys who think elevating a weed growing business eight feet in the air is plenty clandestine enough?

There's probably nothing to worry about. Today's juvenile delinquents are most likely just as smart as yesterday's loiterers. I think I'm just getting old and mean. Frankly, I want this kid to succeed in something other than converting my garage to a greenhouse. I hope he turns it around. Anything is possible. Take it from a guy who was arrested for simply standing: when you do something moronic, there's nowhere to go but up.

GENTRIFICATION VIA BOLOGNA SANDWICH

All around him, the crowd of a few hundred hushes. They form a dense semi-circled pocket. The man in question adjusts his stance, feels for wind and lines up his club. The only sound is a cracking beer can until he swings with the strength of a hammer meeting a wall stud.

His name is Kenny and he isn't golfing. Not even close. We're in Schnitzelburg and Kenny and dozens of others are playing a game called dainty. They've been playing for 41 years. I'd like to hope they'll play for another 41 years, but people like me might be snuffing out all the fun without even knowing it.

The World Dainty Championship is held each summer in this tiny Louisville, KY neighborhood. The area is filled with shotgun houses and local-centric bars. Chances are, it's the only place on earth the game is still played. Inexplicably, the championship is always held on a Monday and always at about 5pm. Not exactly tee time at Augusta. But dainty is nothing like golf, which is no big deal except for one thing. And that thing is a shame.

The shame is that this charming ribbon of Schnitzelburg history will probably soon disappear.

It depresses the hell out of me.

But I'm not depressed at first. Because, while I'm there, the Dainty Championship is a blast. It reminds me of my childhood, growing up in a small town and making up games to entertain ourselves.

Here's the scoop on dainty: guys like Kenny lay a five-inch wooden peg on the street and, with one arm, swing a three-foot wooden broomstick at the peg. One arm is the rule, no exceptions. A successful start will see the little peg popped into the air and spinning wildly. Step Two then has the player swing the broom like a bat and try to knock the peg as far is it'll go.

The street is closed off and every five feet has a spray painted line. The contestants, like Kenny, who are dainty experts crouch low and clip the small peg with precision not seen since Pat Morita catching flies with chopsticks. Like that Hollywood moment, age and patience are the key. In fact, age is a rule in Schnitzelburg. Dainty players *must* be over age 45 to compete.

A successful at-bat fills the air with a wood-on-wood crack that is more satisfying than hearing a triple in baseball.

Kenny is long and lean, balding with big black glasses. Kenny might be pushing retirement age, but you'd never know it after his turn clocked in at a whopping 83 feet. Frankly, in the hour or so I spent there, it was one of the few that made it *anywhere*. Dainty, if you didn't imagine from the above description, seems impossibly hard to master.

But when you do master it, like Kenny, you must feel five, not 45. For the time I was there, standing safely at the 120-foot mark, he is a celebrity. "Hey, this is Kenny," a woman says, introducing him. "He's the leader. He hit 83 feet!"

Frankly, I was almost more impressed that someone didn't know Kenny. Because, while this little slice of neighborhood fun is interesting, what's more interesting is the neighborhood itself. Schnitzelburg is a small town slid inconspicuously into the city's Germantown neighborhood. That, itself, is nothing special. But it's the feel you get riding around its 10 or so blocks. Everyone genuinely seems to know one another. Not in a cul-de-sac *wave at your neighbor* kind of way, but in an honest way. A familiarity that says the people here grew up in this neighborhood and know each other's family history, where they work and what their favorite menu item is at the local grille, Check's.

Chief among these residents is the contest's MC.

Of equal dainty-playing age, the MC stalks the playing field's painted lines. He's boxed in on two sides by orange snow fence that keeps the spectators on the sidewalk. The MC announces the next contestant, usually tossing in a casual, unrehearsed bit that makes me wish I was his buddy, too. "Up next, hey, Foxy Roxy the karaoke queen." The MC announces when players have struck out (players get three swings to knock the peg into the field) and hollers out measurements all with his wireless mic.

And it's that familiarity that makes me love this lower-middle class niche of the city. Schnitzleburg residents have their own bars and restaurants. They all take pride in keeping their homes nice. They mostly all have deeper southern accents than the rest of the city for some anthropologically mystifying reason. Schnitzelburg reminds me of my own microscopic hometown. It's the kind of closeness and community I've seen fabricated so many times with great failure.

The reason this doesn't fail is easy: Because Schnitzleburg has always been this way. Since before they held the World Dainty Championship and before its sponsor, Hauck's Market, opened 100 years ago (**Wentastic Fact**: I went into the aged general store once to get a candy bar. It's the kind of place with raw wood floors and dust covering the Snickers. An old man was sitting by the door, drinking a Budweiser and holding a cane) this neighborhood has had this amazingly warm, tight, community.

But people like me are threatening it.

I didn't realize it at first, but once I did, that's when the Dainty Championship stopped being fun. That's when I wanted to go home and turn down the lights and drink.

The spark that lit this guilty fire inside me was, oddly, bologna sandwiches. For the Championship, Hauck's offers a meal deal— for $1.50 you can have a bologna sandwich, dill pickle and a bag of chips. Hauck's, supposedly, is known for its bologna on white. Longtime Schnitzelburgers were enjoying the delicacies in every direction.

The only people not eating one, it seemed, were people like me. And that distinction is where the danger starts.

The crowd is made up of a lot of guys in mustaches—young fellas rocking them ironically and Schnitzelburg residents who've worn them for decades. A lot of young guys are sporting cutoff jean shorts, probably because they'd seen a band or someone from New York doing it. Schnitzelburg guys wear jean shorts because, well, it's hot. There are a lot of tattoos as well. Young dudes with tatted up, brightly inked arms are mixed against men with faded ink from military service or street gangs long forgotten in favor of domesticity. So similar, but still, not so much. All this comes to a head with bologna. Hauck's is selling it cheap, because it is tasty and costs nothing and people like it. Meanwhile, across the street, a new restaurant is also slinging a bologna sandwich. However, this new joint, owned and operated by people roughly my age and cultural background, are fixing dishes that pay tribute to the neighborhood's German heritage with chic, gourmet flair.

Pretty cool, right? A real help to the community. A positive boost of neighborhood adrenaline, yeah? But they charge nearly ten times as much as Hauck's. Their bologna is from farm-raised, organic pork, situated between a brioche bun and served with sides like chilled barley salad. Not a pickle or bag of wavy chips in sight. Real Schnitzers wouldn't be caught dead here.

And right there, on plates filled with bologna, is why this wonderful little tradition is going to die. And, in all likelihood, this charming, warm neighborhood will get a pine box all its own. People like me are to blame.

We're not trying to ruin Schnitzelburg, but we are anyway. We are 20- and 30-something and looking to buy our first home and live close to the heart of the city. Germantown and Schnitzelburg offers Louisville's most affordable homes, short of places where bullets and meth fly through the air.

Everyone is friendly. But the long-time residents don't talk to the newcomers pushing fancy jogger strollers. We're all segregated, watching dainty players trying to avoid that massive oak tree that hangs over the street, gobbling up little wooden pegs like comic strip kites. We just don't have much in common, aside from location.

The Kroger down the street is jumping on the bandwagon. It once featured cracked linoleum floors, stacks of light domestic beers and bottles of teriyaki sauce that were probably years out of date. The store expanded and remodeled and now has faux-wood flooring, an extensive microbrew selection and a really nice Asian foods department with, like, four different kinds of curry. They're doing this because people at my station in life love (oddly) pushing carts over hardwoods, debating the merits of the world's IPAs and Thai food. And Schnitzelberg will keep shifting this way. There's no stopping its momentum.

Because, as dainty players move further and further beyond age 45, young people looking for cheap housing will continue to populate the neighborhood. We're not exploiting anyone and really, opening a hip German-heritage restaurant is good for the area. Soon, nobody will remember how to play dainty and nobody'll know that Foxy Roxy is the karaoke queen, because when Check's is replaced by a Belgian beer bar, they won't want someone belting out Heart's greatest hits.

There will be no MC to encourage us to clap for Kenny "You know, Zap Parker's boy" because nobody'll know anyone else.

We don't mean to ruin the neighborhood. We're just being ourselves, but in the process, we're snuffing out something wonderful and warm.

BABIES WHO LISTEN TO MEGADETH...

I am not yet a father.

We have a baby kid on the way in November. So it's a technicality, really. However, over the last year I have kept a diary. I made a lot of entries. Way too many to be exact. But let's face it, nobody wants to read my musings on what onesie colors will help produce an NBA small forward. So, I have condensed my thoughts into a tidy, Eagles *Greatest Hits* version of a diary.

July 1, 2010
[Email to Medved, asking for fathering advice.]
Me: Hey dude, Leah and I are getting more serious about having one of these babies I keep hearing everyone talk about. I'm not positive, but they're kind of like an HD TV or something, right?

Medved: Babies are like an HD TV, only with higher resale value on the black market. Oh, and they poop.

August 19, 2010
Lying in bed.

Leah has to start her pills in two days. It's time to figure out if we are serious about babies. We decide, since it takes a few months for birth control to get of your system, she will stop. Sounds kind of like dudes in high school trying to pass a drug test...maybe if she drinks pickle juice it'll flush out of her body faster?

September 14, 2010

Twice in one week I have failed to get it up. Why? Part of me feels a strange pressure, like there is a job I must do. And, like all responsibilities I'm asked to take on—from doing the dishes, to getting a real job, to shaving at least once a week—I ultimately blow it.

October 6, 2010

We've been together now for 11 years and damn near every time we had sex before, I was full of anxiety about getting Leah pregnant.

Now, I am full of anxiety over whether I *can* get her pregnant.

Somewhere, the 19-year-old version of myself is high-fiving someone.

October 18, 2010

A doctor told Bob *[my father-in-law]* he has a year to live, cancer is in his blood.

It's a disorienting feeling—not panic, little sadness, just a lot of numb rationality. Why is that?

Also strange because Leah has been getting sick lately. She took a pregnancy test this morning. Negative. But if not, how utterly strange that would be.

--

My grandma is 91, and for 90 of those years she's been named Norma.

She was nameless for her first year of life, she just told me.

Finally, her parents decided to name her after the neighbor girl, exactly like the neighbor girl: Norma Anita. I can't imagine that happening today without a restraining order being filed.

Oddly, Grandma told another story about an older guy in town named Baby Boy Flores. Apparently, his folks thought the hospital did everyone a service and named babies for you. So when they left and his birth certificate said, "Baby Boy Flores," it stuck.

*[There is a huge gap in entries because trying to have a baby didn't turn out to be the mid-90s warehouse rave we thought it was going to be. So writing about our failures—such as my aforementioned floppiness issues, coupled with my wife not getting a period due to the stress of Bob's

illness—was kind of depressing.]

March 7, 2011
[After much confusion at the doctor's office over an ovarian cyst, it is discovered Leah is indeed pregnant. Yes, I got over my case of Wet Noodle Fever, thanks for asking.]

Is this who I thought I would be when I would someday father a child: 31, greasy-haired, smelling in need of a shower and making less money than I did at Wal-Mart in high school?

No, this is not who I imagined I would be.

For one, this whole process doesn't happen in a montage sequence featuring the sounds of Alice in Chains; secondly, I am not on tour with some incredibly popular, but still indie-cred heavy band; third, I do not own a hoverboard.

--

This time *[The hazy days prior to the 12 week safe point when miscarriage risks drop]* is like discovering a varmint under the house. It's definitely in there, I can see something…but I don't know what it is.

Is it going to stay?

Will it just pack up and disappear unannounced some night?

Should I leave it a plate of table scraps?

March 9, 2011
Bob has been placed in hospice. Even though it is too early to be telling people, we shared the news with Leah's mom and Bob. He is on so many medications it's hard to know if he understood. I imagine somewhere he hears.

March 16, 2011
Bob died today. We were in the room with him. It's dizzying, learning within a week that we are having a baby and then losing someone close.

March 24, 2011

Leah is officially six-and-a-half weeks along and we got this early preview because of the cyst on her ovaries. The doctor was primarily checking that little bubble out, but took a sharp left turn to provide a peek at Little Billy Ocean. (For whatever reason, we've begun calling this child Billy Ocean. This is a step up from the *Arrested Development* reference "Gene Parmesan" that was in vogue around the house for a while.)

Billy is about the size of a seed. We could see his little heart fluttering. Which was pretty much all there was. This makes him a perfect Wensink: All heart and no brains.

April 12, 2011

Leah's baby names are okay, but I think I have a flair for this. My favorite suggestions:

- Baron Von Wensink. Or Baron Vaughn Wensink.

- Cannon Ball Wensink

- Admiral Wensink

- Archibald Duke Wensink (AKA Archduke Wensink)

May 19, 2011

We've finally been telling friends about the baby. The best response was from Kassie at the Decemberists concert: "Congratulations! Wait…it's on purpose right?"

--

I'm convinced there are no materials [book, video or otherwise] catering to the father-to-be who didn't accidentally get someone pregnant on a Carnival cruise.

Everything is worded to tell me: "Hey dude, so you're not too psyched about that little human getting in the way of your lady's pussy. Bummer, I know. But, okay, you gotta play it cool and man up. Chicks dig that."

June 3, 2011

Leah went to the store and purchased more pillows. She has them strategically placed on the bed, much like my boyhood forts. The results for her sleeping comfort are better, but sort of claustrophobic as it leaves me about eight inches of bed space. On the plus side, I now have no fear of death, because most coffins provide roomier accommodations.

June 24, 2011

Every guy I see on the street juggling fire or reciting poetry is a reminder that I need to give our kid a lot of hugs.

--

Last Friday we had our ultrasound. It's a boy! Walter Wensink it is. He was sideways in the image so we got a profile of his body and all you could see was a skull and a spine. He looked like a dinosaur. A Waltersaurus.

July 1, 2011

Every father is nervous. He is nervous because there will soon be this human who depends on you for love, shelter and food. And that human will someday not share your taste in rap music.

--

Read *being-a-dad* book chapter that wasn't total horseshit. It was about talking to babies before they are born. Apparently, it helps them recognize who you are out of the womb. Plus, music and books make them, like, little geniuses.

So, I began talking to Walter. A neighbor was blasting off firecrackers, and I explained how awesome fireworks are. Also, I decided to do a little self-promotion and explained that in the real world I am considered the handsomest man alive. Also, I am unbeatable in bench presses and 40 yard dashes.

July 7, 2011

Leah suspects she felt a kick. Not sure. She says it's: "You know, like when milk doesn't settle well in your belly."

I have no idea what she is talking about.

We've also been playing Vivaldi in hopes Walter will grow up incredibly smart, like a doctor, politician or cat burglar.

July 15, 2011

If you do not have a vagina, you are dead to the doctor. Here's a good example:

ME: So, we've been playing music and talking to the baby. Is there any volume that is too loud? I don't want to hurt his hearing—

DOCTOR: No. (Looks at me like I just wet my pants)

--

Lying on a hammock yesterday, I realized with some sadness that my hammock-lying days are numbered.

July 25, 2011

FACT: 7 out of 10 babies who are played Megadeth are born with mustaches.

August 8, 2011

Today we learned what the word "Triage" means. We honestly didn't know eight hours ago.

This last weekend we went down to Lake Kentucky with our friends. The boat ride was surprisingly choppy, smacking the water and flooding the floor. This worried me and eventually hit Leah as a worry, too. The big problem was that Walter didn't really kick or move afterward and a weird stomach pain developed. Worse, Leah researched boating while pregnant and (much like playing volleyball, getting in a car wreck or doing your taxes) discovered that the online community thinks this could pretty much kill our baby. Detach the placenta from the uterus, I believe.

We called the doctor this morning and they said to go to triage. (Side note: Leah kept asking people, "What exactly is the triage?" **Nurse:** "Oh, you know, it's where you go in and they triage your belly." Ah, thanks for clarifying!)

Walter is fine it turns out. We got scared for nothing. But was it nothing? For a handful of hours I felt miserable. It reminded me of the ugly emotions back when we thought maybe we couldn't have a baby at all. It's an intense, lonely, sinking. The mind wanders—will she have to deliver a stillborn baby? Will we bury it? Will we buy a very small headstone?

Such a brutal sadness.

It served, thankfully, as a reminder of how far we've come. It's incredible to see our love for this guy and he's not even here yet. It's a sign of what our life would look like without a Walter. No thanks.

I have not even begun dreaming of the millions he'll bring in as a baby model/child actor/diaper-tester and I am still concerned for his safety. Father of the Year, here I come.

August 10, 2011

Walter's room is painted. I built his crib last night. One tool the Million Dollar Baby Corporation failed to mention in its instruction manual: (1) Manhattan on the rocks.

Without it, I might have tossed the entire operation into the trash. Ah, but with bourbon, I was calm and focused. Perhaps hard booze will become a handy parenting tool, too?

August 11, 2011

Sympathy pain I understand.

Sympathy weight gain even makes sense.

But Sympathy sagging?

Must be true. I've noticed my pectorals look like boobs when I wear t-shirts. This never happened before. It must be the pregnancy, right? Either that or I haven't even sniffed a weight bench since 1998.

BOOB JOB

My son is due to arrive sometime in November. Since my wife and I have no child raising experience beyond her lucrative babysitting gig in 1994, we figured we should learn the basics.

We've been reading baby books that gently scare us to sleep each night with visions of spinal meningitis and SIDS and warnings against giving baby Walter sweet-ass dragon tattoos before age five. Luckily, our hospital also offers free seminars for expectant parents. The first one we signed up for was Breastfeeding 101.

I pictured some calm collection of plump-bellied ladies and their doting daddies sitting in a circle, learning about that miracle of miracles: free baby food.

Instead, we were boxed into a massive conference room that reminded me of a tricky timeshare shakedown Leah and I once attended in Portland, OR, promising a free trip to Vegas. This room, instead, had free graham crackers and apple juice. The walls were bare and the tables were sterile and the scrub-clad lactation consultant led us via PowerPoint presentation. The setup felt like the days before I was a professional writer, back when I had a real job at a life insurance company. I spent most of the two hour session in a sprinter's position, ready to bolt at the first mention of "accidental death and dismemberment," "team synergy" or "getting traction on this new project."

Luckily, the entire seminar was helpful and informative. So informative, I actually took notes. Below is a verbatim transcription of my notes from Breastfeeding 101.

• Strong foods like chili and burritos can flavor breast milk 4-6 hours after eating. Yum! Best of both worlds, eh, Walter?

• Apparently, the baby is not big enough to fend for itself until it's been in the womb 39 weeks.

NOTE TO SELF: Buy Walter a switchblade if he is born early.

• Man, how many nipples has this lactation consultant seen? More than a porn director? I bet way more than a porn director.

• According to the lactation consultant, for the first hour after childbirth we go to some place called "Kangaroo Care." If there's not a bouncy pit I will be pissed.

• If the baby pinches the nipple while feeding, mom is supposed to use her pinky and press down on his tongue to get him to unlatch…and if that doesn't work, swat him with a rolled newspaper, saying: "No!" and "Bad!"

• This breastfeeding how-to movie is like some Cold War-era CIA brainwashing technique—it broke my spirit. I never want to see another nipple as long as I live. I will give you my name, rank and serial number.

• Dear Producer of this Breastfeeding Movie:

That's enough Rosie O'Donnell look-alikes, thank you.

- According to the lactation consultant, we are not supposed to use a microwave or bottle warmer to heat chilled milk. So, I'm assuming that means stir frys are okay?

NOTE TO SELF: Put a wok on the baby shower registry.

HONEY, THIS BABY IS BROKEN
OR SOME SHIT

I became a stay-at-home-dad for one reason: the pussy.

It wasn't because I'm a writer and am already home all day anyways. It wasn't to save money since daycare costs as much as Notre Dame tuition. And it certainly wasn't after reading that one study about how kids with a parent at home end up something like 75% less likely to rob a bank.

I volunteered for that most noble of fatherly duties: because of its potential to tap some serious ass while my wife's at work.

Society has told me there is a light at the end of the tunnel of pooped diapers and sticky vomit. And that light is shaped like a vulva.

It's a fact: women love a guy with a baby.

Pretty much every man on the parental fence knows, in the back of his head, hot girls will magically start flirting once that kid arrives. It's what seals the fatherhood deal most of the time. In fact, close inspection of the Baby Bjorn owner's manual shows that the world's finest uncomfortable papoose-looking thingy was created to specifically aid a stay-at-home-dad's quest for Wednesday afternoon oral.

Or, so I was led to believe.

Now I realize the stereotype of a father's irresistibility was nothing more than a clever double-fakeout. A feminine ploy for free nannying.

For a long time I just figured our baby was busted. Or worse... ugly.

But that's not possible.

For starters, Walter has my nose and his mom's blue eyes and these adorable chubby cheeks. My kid is the Ryan Gosling of four-month-olds. And yet, book-sexy lasses at the library ignore me when I say "Daddy loves you" in that silly voice Walter enjoys and kiss his forehead. Skinny jeaned girls at the grocery store don't even try to make-out after I tickle his chin in the vegetable aisle. Not once has an attractive runner in a sports bra offered a handjob while I push the stroller down a sidewalk. Even though it's perfectly good handjob weather.

No, my kid isn't defective. He's not sex-repellent. The baby is not the problem. The problem is society tricking legions of men into staying home and raising their own children.

The epiphany arrived one morning before the sun was anywhere near up—scooping Similac into a bottle, head throbbing for coffee that'll have to wait until Junior is fed, changed and chilled out. Obviously, women have been lying to me! The promise of unlimited booty was just a mirage. While my wife is off having the time of her life at the office, I'm stuck at the house with no hope of an illicit affair.

How else can I explain my strange lack of extra-marital acrobatics? It's pretty clear women never found it adorable that grown men were lugging around kids. This is just a scam that sticks papa with all the responsibility while mom's probably getting nails painted or some hair waxed while sipping mimosas and laughing about our monogamous genitals.

By my calculations, decades-worth of ladies have been paying it forward, propagating this rumor: "yes, we think it's irresistible when a guy takes care of a baby." All the while, they've had no intention of ever sexing me up. The entire female species has tricked me into caring for my own son.

Nice try ladies—I'm on to you.

But it's your lucky day, this secret is safe. True, I could take this bombshell to Congress or FOX News or the suddenly unsexy dad-n-lad Thursday playgroup. But, I won't.

Why?

Because, single ladies and your vaginas, the joke's on you. Our fragile little treaty will remain unshattered for now, because I kind of like wearing sweat pants and not shaving and smelling this way.

And, yes, don't even say it. I know there's a stain on my shirt. It's spitup from *yesterday*'s lunch.

Get one last look, because it's all for my wife. Tough luck.

I STOLE FROM KIDS

It was going to be beautiful, like Butch and Sundance wearing Baby Bjorns.

The stay-at-home-dad Bonnie and Clyde, except both of us Clyde.

Two stealthy bandits, quick on the teething ring draw.

But, as they say, *the best laid plans to rob children...*

We had every intention of plucking their property and that was enough. Just discovering one owns the nasty blood needed to steal from boys too young for armpit hair does something. It makes the manliest, most-glamorous job on Earth—house husband—turn a little sour.

It started when the lousy neighbor kids stopped shooting hoops and started tossing rocks over our fence, nearly hitting my six-month-old son. Out in the alley, full of overgrown grass and gravel and shattered bottles, I confronted the boys beneath the rim. This was our third such conversation. Eyes bulging, I basically said, "Knock it off!" at top volume.

"Leave me alone. You're making me mad. Jeez," a freckled, redheaded rock-tosser, maybe 12, told me. I repeated my radical views on infanticide, but Red simply walked away, unintimidated by some angry dude with spit-up stains on his shirt.

Sigh.

A man's masculinity loses its gloss when he can't even convince a little boy to stop trying to hurt a baby.

That man—let's just hypothetically call him *me*—might see this as the cherry atop his emasculation sundae. Hard not to draw that conclusion, what with babysitting all day while my wife earns roughly triple my meager book royalties and freelance pay.

But, standing in the alley, watching Red dribble off, I was inspired to nip this neighborhood nuisance at the source. I immediately realized I have no scruples stealing from children when it came to my son's safety. Maybe I needed excuses to inject some testosterone into a routine now dominated by Diaper Genies, tummy-time and generally operating like Aunt Bee with stubble.

Maybe.

"Just call the police," my wife suggested.

"Talk to his parents," a friend said.

"Ignore him," my mother said.

Easy for them. They weren't imagining baby Walter's shattering squeal when rock meets face. That awful dream repeated the following day, growing loud enough to leave tinnitus. The plan was simple: reclaim my manhood by swiping the pillar of kid-related alley activity. Goodbye, basketball hoop.

The boys used it every day, but, best I could tell, the bucket belonged to nobody. Like an Easter Island sculpture, historians were unclear when the hoop arrived in the alley. Some said prehistoric times, some claimed turn of the century, others remember it arriving unannounced two months back.

The basket looked as if it were part of an archeological gymnasium excavation. It had no net, was coated with dirt and rust, and weighed down by a jagged clump of concrete. If that basketball hoop were a frontier child, it would be the first eaten by wolves.

Perhaps, a wolf suffering from stroller bursitis.

I recruited my pickup-owning pal, Jeremy, who is also a stay-at-home-dad. As opposed to a predictable midnight mission, we'd go hoop-napping at noon. The alley was a ghost town at lunch since everyone but baby daddies works or is at school.

This burglaring lifestyle was thrilling. "It's a victimless crime!" I told Jeremy at the park as we pushed our sons in swings. I was very proud of my elegant solution.

No hoop = no kids = no rock-throwing = no baby Cyclops.

"Okay," Jeremy said. "Whatever, man. Sounds good." While he seemed ambivalent, I had enough misguided rage for two. "Just let me know when to bring the truck over."

Hours later, after careful calculations during naptime, I texted

Jeremy that tomorrow would be Heist Day. It also asked, "Is your wife off? Otherwise, we'll have to get a sitter for the boys."

Prior to my career in diaper rash extermination, I was too bogged down with morality to steal anything, especially children's toys. That me was long gone as the pride of keeping my son safe, surprisingly, drowned guilt with a firm hand.

I was really liking this new me. He was a go-getter!

That's when tragedy struck.

The next morning, I discovered some enterprising Howard Carter a few houses down claimed King Tut's mummified hoop for himself, wheeling the remains into their driveway. I dashed Jeremy an emergency text: "Mission aborted. Hoop moved. Shit, I'm sad."

Days later, I was still edgy. I couldn't puree sweet potatoes or sing the ABCs without grinding my teeth. I was obsessed over missed opportunities, even though I got what I wanted. The rock tossers had vanished. Yet, part of me ached to drag the basket back to the alley, just for the thrill of stealing it.

That new me was a go-getter, but also angry and quasi-amoral. Why?

That me arrived, I realized, because there's a heavy shadow sitting atop we house husbands.

No matter how much you love your kid (and I do, he's my best friend) there's a not-so-fresh feeling with home-daddery. Simply put, it's impossible to be the man of the house while sporting a polka dot diaper bag. There's also a great deal of unintended frustration with this job. Maybe it's because our ladies are bringing home more bacon. Maybe it's spending free time folding onesies instead of looking at dirty pictures online like days long gone. Most likely it's just our inability to produce milk.

Eventually, the anger evaporated. Red and his rocks triggered a major overreaction because I couldn't cope with home-daddy's place in the world. Actually, I probably should have simply shot hoops with the kids instead of plotting against them. I think I could use the stress release of exercise.

MY BABY BEAT MY ASS

I cut off mom's thumb.

Or so the story goes.

I was a toddler playing with scissors and she went to snatch them but got caught in the line of fire. According to family legend: the thumb was dangling by a tendon. Her appendage only works today thanks to some miracle of early-80s finger surgery.

But today the scar looks like a flesh wound at best. I mean, how bad could it have really been? Mom didn't even press charges.

But, the myth's been made and it'll live forever as-is. I should be so lucky with my kid.

"Is this the guy who beat you up?" one nurse asks.

"There's the big, mean bully," another giggles.

"You poor thing."

I expected teasing after I phoned the doctor's office, explained my malady, and heard nothing but laughs between the receptionist's clenched teeth. The nurses are poking fun at me, not the baby. Walter gets off the hook because he's chubby and cute and seven months old. His father became the butt of the doctor's office's jokes shortly after they opened this morning. "I think I have a broken nose," I said on the phone.

"How did that happen?" the receptionist asked.

"I'm pretty sure my baby broke it."

Commence snickering.

I'm no Olympic bench pressing judge or anything, but Walter is freakishly strong. He never really had that Jell-O-neck phase like most babies. He's pretty much always been able to hold his massive head (95ᵗʰ percentile, if you must know) by himself. This itty-bitty brute force has recently translated into problems: the boy's rippled with baby muscles, but has no control over them.

My son is a tiny Kool-Aid Man and the world is his brick wall.

At least once a day he swings that massive skull back into my face or socks me in the eye or nose. It hurts. If a drunk buddy accidentally thumped me this hard, I'd clock his arm for good measure.

But Walter is 20 pounds of misguided musculature. Plus, he's chubby and cute. I can't get mad. Even when he makes Daddy the story all the nurses will tell their significant others at dinner tonight: "This one guy came in today, get this, his *baby* kicked his ass!"

I'm not angry at them, either. My son did whoop my ass…more specifically, my nose. It stung to the touch, was red and swelling like famous lying marionettes. According to late night online medical searches, I owned a broken nose.

Walter: 1

Daddy: 0

The doctor, thankfully, didn't get her degree from *Web M.D.* "Well," she says, shining a light up my snout, while Daddy's Little Nose-Crusher sits on my lap. "It's not broken."

Relief should be flooding in, but instead I am disappointed.

With a flick of her penlight, the doc has ruined one of the best stories of my life. Equal, if not better, than scissoring off mom's thumb. I was already crafting the details of how the fruit of my loins shattered my nose. It would become the gold standard of Wensink Family Lore.

My nose is not a point of pride. It's the strangest feature on a face filled with Photoshop-like distortions. I was perfectly comfortable breaking it for the pleasure of constructing a thrilling Dad vs. Lad saga.

Instead, I'm left with nothing but a nasal staph infection and a prescription for antibiotics. It's a shame, because those tall tales are all I'll have when my career as a house husband ends. I need good raw materials to build with.

So much family joy comes from exaggerating the truth.

Myth-making keeps memories fresh. Exaggeration vacuum seals our experience into a brick of astronaut ice cream. Nobody talks about the cloth diapers and colic mom dealt with. We talk about her thumb. The story stays alive and reminds us of the insane sacrifice parents make. Something deep within me craved that broken nose because nobody'll share anecdotes at future Thanksgivings about the gallons of Desitin I smeared across He-Man Jr.'s rump.

Even worse, we'll someday forget the endless blog posts documenting first steps, first words and first really weird poops. In all likelihood, the hundreds of JPEGs we've taken will grow outdated and unviewable one day. Walter's too little to remember and my wife is at work. So, these domestic tall tales are all I have to document time as a stay-at-home-dad. With any luck those stories might just help me live forever. I mean, "staph infection" sounds pretty dangerous, right?

Hmmmm.

Maybe it's time to finally let a certain cute, chubby seven-month old play with scissors?

THE SWEATIEST CORPSE

It is the hottest day of summer so far, well over three digits, and you are dead.

You are lying on the blacktop with a Honda Civic covering half of your body. The ground is an oven's heating coil against your back and arm and head—turning them each a sunburn color. And you are dead.

Supposed to be dead, anyhow.

Other cadavers are flopped into the grass, aching to itch themselves, one girl is slumped against a door, one man is facedown on the sidewalk. You can't see them, your eyes are closed because you are awesome at being dead.

But being awesome means you are the sweatiest corpse in history.

This, you guess, is what they call *Hollywood Magic*.

How many movies have you watched—you wonder, as the sun pounds heavy and the tree leaves hiss—with a heap of bodies lying around? The bloody trail of a monster film, the carnage of war pictures, piles of plague victims doing whatever it was they were doing when the Big Moment came. You never appreciated how much work it was to be dead until you, yourself, were forced into service.

The director yells "cut" and you sit up to feel your flesh throb. It's a refreshing few moments until his voice yells out that we have to do it again, "places," "quiet on the set," "action."

You volunteered. You told the directors you'd help with the movie any way, shape or form. And now you get to be dead. Which, actually, will be pretty cool when all this is over. But for now it's hotter than expected and every bead of sweat darkens your outlook.

The 48 Hour Film Festival rolled into town this week and your two friends, aspiring movie-makers, asked for help. The idea is that we draw a genre from a hat, get a randomly assigned prop, character and line of dialogue on Friday night and submit a finished movie on Sunday evening. Your team, calling itself Yellow Umbilical Cord Productions for reasons unknown, stayed up until two in the morning Friday to whip up a five page script for the *thriller* genre. In the film, scientists are quarantined because of a plague, but rations are running low inside the bunker and people keep ending up murdered. It ain't *Waiting for Godot*, but it's a lot of fun.

Fun, that is, until you died. Until you entered the spirit world soaking with sweat.

You've been on set for 10 hours already, living on little sleep, and it never occurred to you how hard it is to make pretend. Six minutes of film time will take almost 12 hours to shoot. The final thing the directors need is an exterior shot showcasing the pile of bodies around the bunker. That's where a Honda Civic ran you over, leaving you to bake like a loaf of sourdough until the director says, "cut."

This is a lot of hard work. You never thought about how much effort goes into lighting someone's face: up to half an hour, just to get things set right. And how delicate it is to frame a shot—countless minutes of looking and thinking and rearranging. We are all amateurs here and it is difficult and time-consuming. It makes you wonder how movies ever get finished at all.

How long did it take three *Godfathers* to be shot, you wonder as you fry. For that matter, jeez, what about that one Hungarian movie, *Satantango*, that is seven hours long? If it took your group 12 hours to film six minutes, that's a couple of years of this stuff. How many times did they have to hit reset when someone stumbled on a line, or a dog barked in the background or a sweaty dead body's chest was jumping up and down from heat exhaustion?

Maybe that was just you.

But there you are when the man behind the camera yells "cut" one last time and the corpses stand and breathe sighs of relief and compare scorch marks. The director apologizes and the day is done. Your little movie is made, mostly, except for the editing, color correction and music that must be added before the 48 hours are up.

Driving home with your wife, who played a corpse with a broken umbrella, you are looking forward to renting a movie soon. Films will not look the same because now that you have died you can see into some limbo that exists between the DVD and your perception of make believe. You won't be able to watch even the dumbest sequel without a warm appreciation for how much work went into production. You'll say things like, "Wow, *House Party 3* is ninety-minutes long. That'd take us nearly four years to film. Good job, Kid 'N' Play!"

Even the smallest detail took so much focus and cooperation. You had to come back from the dead to see things that were always hiding right in front of your eyes. This prickly, detailed world full of energy. Hey, that sandwich baggie commercial was probably a lot of work, I never thought about the guy who holds a microphone for the newscasters. And so on and so on.

And by the time you get home, grits of blacktop still sticking to your burial clothes, skin throbbing a little less, you wonder: what else have you been missing? How many other little invisible elements make up the world around you? It's amazing, you think, how being dead opens your eyes.

AIDING AND ABIDING AT
THE LEBOWSKI FEST

"Step right up! Only a dollar, folks," my voice booms through an electric megaphone. "Toss the dirty undies.

"Hit a nihilist.

"Help the kids."

I am at a bowling alley parking lot with the summer sun setting in my face, cooking it pink. I am sweaty and regret not wearing shorts. Luckily, the crowd doesn't notice.

"All proceeds go to charity. C'mon, ladies and gentlemen. Toss the Ringer. Toss the Ringer. Toss the Ringer."

People are wearing costumes, elaborate costumes, in every direction. Only infrequently do they pay attention to the guy barking through a bullhorn. I'm failing miserably and simultaneously letting down disadvantaged children. Nice work, Wensink.

Until...

"They believe in *nothing*, show them you believe in *something*."

Heads turn a little, a few chuckles poke from the passing crowd. Suddenly, I don't feel like a sweaty buffoon. Now I'm just sweaty. Slowly, an audience forms because of those simple words.

I am a sort-of carnival barker at the 10th Annual Lebowski Fest in Louisville, Kentucky. A two day love-a-thon of all things *Big Lebowski*. Spinning the, "we believe in nothing," line to my own advantage is the sort of quote-dropping folks expect. It's a line Chili Peppers bassist, Flea, and the other nihilists in the film turned into magic. And sure enough, its magic brings in contestants. A guy dressed like a buzz-shorn Vietnam vet—the spitting image of John

Goodman's character—sticks out a dollar. My wife takes the buck and adds it to the pot.

Cheers rise wildly, drowning my bullhorn. The crowd is sweaty, too, but couldn't be happier than to watch a guy toss old underpants through the air.

This little sideshow, called The Ringer Toss, boasts a perfect replica of Jeff Lebowski's rusted green 1972 Plymouth Fury. Our little contest features a bowling bag full of dirty underwear—"the whites" many people scream, further quoting the flick. Contestants are reenacting a scene from the Cohen Brothers' cult film by tossing the Ringer. Onscreen, the Ringer was supposed to be a bowling bag stuffed with money, but Goodman's Walter character swapped out the cash with his unwashed undergarments.

But at the Lebowski Fest, what is supposed to be a bowling bag of dirty underwear is, in fact…a bowling bag of dirty underwear.

The object of the game is to throw the satchel out the passenger side window, over the car roof and hit the leather-clad mannequin (wearing a Nixon mask) with the bag, thus fusing together a later scene in the film. Flea must be busy, so plastic Tricky Dick is our stand-in nihilist.

Walter's real name is Luke, and he traveled from Dallas. "Let's hear it for Walter," I shout into the megaphone. People clap, people yell, people smile. "Walter-Walter-Walter," I chant and people repeat. We're one big, happy weirdo family. *Maybe,* I think, *those orphans won't go lonely tonight. Nice work, Wensink.*

Luke from Dallas hucks the briefs end-over-end and clocks Nixon in the nose, collapsing its entire body like when Wicked Witches meet water. "All right!" I scream, "let's hear it for Walter! Don't forget to collect your prize." His grand prize for hitting an inanimate object with stained BVDs: a 25-cent box of snap pops.

Such is the Lebowski Fest. Inane fun for the sake of inane fun. And for a decade, they've done it better than anybody.

You'd be forgiven for not knowing about this event. But a good Louisville citizen will fix that problem swiftly, telling anyone who'll listen about our annual gathering of costumed silliness. People from Louisville are proud of the Lebowski Fest. Mainly because it's a good time. But also because satellite events have sprung up around the globe from New York, to Portland, to England. The Fest has a sterling reputation among dirty underwear aficionados. Folks, like Luke, travel from all over. I asked Hanes-tossers and heard "Arkansas," "Long Island," "Florida," and beyond.

Louisvillians of a certain age mention the Fest in the same breath as the Kentucky Derby, Muhammad Ali and baseball bats—all hometown originals. The Lebowski weekend involves, of course, watching the movie. And it finishes with bowling and costume contests (people do their best to mimic Jeff Bridges, John Turturro, Goodman, Steve Buschemi and others. But, more entertainingly, they also scrap together outfits based on characters from its famed hallucination scenes. Probably most entertaining, others dress as actual quotes, like "Give me the money, Shithead," featuring a woman with poo for a hat walking around with people dressed as $50 bills).

But the inanest of the inane is sandwiched in between the opening and closing: the garden party. Which is where your narrator-slash-carny barker comes in.

The garden party turns the launching of rotten skivvies into a howling good time. There are also booths for marmot tossing and flipping a blowup doll on a trampoline made from a bed sheet, just like Jackie Treehorn's beach party. All gaming proceeds, believe it or not, go to help Big Brothers Big Sisters. Not exactly the Little Lebowski Urban Achievers, but damn close. There is also nonstop action from bands on a Lollapalooza-large stage. My favorite was a group from Cincinnati composed of drums, accordion and banjo.

Somehow, Leah got mixed into the volunteerism. And through another stroke of fortune, I got to tag along. Today, the White Russian gods smiled and the Ringer Toss game needed an MC for an hour. An MC who, apparently, didn't get enough hugs as a child because he's hungry for attention. After Luke takes his trophy, I continue hollering through the horn, struggling to keep the interest of passers-by. This would be hard work even if it weren't the dead of July and I weren't wearing wet laundry. Unfortunately, it is and I am. Several times I hint to the college kid volunteering that he should give the bullhorn a shot—no luck.

Somewhere, big brothers and big sisters and their little orphan buddies are sad again. Nice work, Wensink.

But, slowly, maybe from dropping movie quotes and maybe

because the lady dressed as a bowling pin felt sorry for me, I help build a stack of dollar bills any pole dancer would be proud of.

I even get to meet a celebrity, unbeknownst to me.

Jim Hoosier, the actor who played Turturro's sidekick, Liam, is on hand and tosses in a buck for the cause. We cheer Jim on, but he misses the mark. Undies spill from the bag across the lawn. Only later do I realize Hoosier wasn't just someone dressed as the thick-necked movie bowler, but the guest of honor at this year's Fest. Such is life when costumed fanaticism runs this deep.

When we arrived, I did not pass under the entrance tent with the intention of encouraging others to toss The Whites. And, even though nature's melanoma factory is working overtime today, the nasty sun doesn't stop me from having a good time. Later, cooling down, I can't help but wonder *why*.

Normally, (if you've paid attention to the previous pages in this book) I hate this kind of shit.

The 10th Annual Lebowski Fest is a manufactured *event*. A festival. When visiting State Fairs, conventions, or regional fests I usually can't escape the fact there is a certain sadness all around. There's an aroma of desperation and fakeness in the air at those places.

Today, while working the bullhorn for all it's worth, I would be bummed if this Fest had any affiliation with a movie studio or was sponsored by a hip website or was intended to promote...*anything*. But there is hardly a whiff of consumerism, secret or otherwise. Yes, there are t-shirts and bumper stickers and car air fresheners and baby onesies with Lebowski-centric idioms for sale. And, yes, the admission is kind of high for a bowling alley lawn littered with dirty underwear. Astronomically high if you consider today's entertainment doesn't include any big-name bands or legitimate stars from *The Big Lebowski*.

But, I realize, maybe there's a brilliant Lebowski Logic to it all.

Everything around the ugly green Plymouth is a type of reverse marketing. A sharp way to separate *us* and *them*. For example: when a small town hosts an apple butter festival, it's not really to cherish their local toast spread, but to rake in money and encourage tourism. That's no shocker. But Lebowski Fest's admission fee and lack of marquee entertainment ensures only fellow lovers of silly fun and cult film fetishists attend. It dissuades anyone who would be attracted for any other reason than to simply bask in the glow of fellow obsessives and goofballs. This dramatically shrinks the Lebowski Fest's gene pool and leaves something potent, pure, and fun.

On the whole, the festival isn't trying to sell anything but a goofy good time centered around a movie that has taken on a mystifying life of its own. And that makes the event a surprise. It kind of confuses me at first: attending a big event that doesn't treat its visitors as a wallet with a pulse. That distinction is so subtle I don't even realize it until we've left the bowling alley that night.

I wasn't prepared to be the PT Barnum of skidmarked whites and I wasn't prepared to enjoy it so damn much. And I'm lucky for it. It's surprising what happens when you bring together likeminded lovers of the inane, a big event not selling anything and a bowling satchel filled with dirty underwear—it really ties a room together.

CELEBRATING SIX YEARS OF FAILURE

I've been a failure at every job I've ever held.

You're looking at someone who's been forcibly removed from the premises as a legal assistant, flat-out fired from a children's museum marketing department, and once, preemptively quit a job proofing insurance documents in fear of a pink slip. Plus, I've been ignored-to-death by more freelance copywriting gigs than I can count.

So, when getting my book, *Broken Piano for President*, published started looking like a lot of legitimate work, the writing seemed scrawled across failure's wall.

Thankfully, unlike that door-to-door cell phone sales job in Tucson, I didn't simply walk away during lunch. But the novel's path from first draft to book store shelves features enough disappointment to fill a Republican primary.

People tell me many books, like Don DeLillo's *Underworld* or James Joyce's *Ulysses,* took about six years, too. I don't even try to point out the glaring differences in our three situations.

2006: I work on a draft for months and join a novel writing workshop in Portland, OR. I think this young version of *Broken Piano* is already pretty good. However, my fellow shopmates disagree.

Not enough Orcs, says the guy writing about trolls. It would be better with a tender birthing scene, suggests the lady writing about midwifery. Add a sassy but vulnerable divorcée detective, says... pretty much everyone else.

Such is life at the writing workshop.

Some of the advice is helpful and I now set my sights on an MFA. As most blogs and book jackets tell me, MFAs are the only way to get published unless your parents' last names are Safran and Foer. I apply to 10 schools using *Broken Piano for President* as my writing sample. I am promptly rejected by eight and waitlisted at Columbia College and Pittsburgh. Like a misguided Match.com date, these prospects soon stop pretending they're interested.

2007: I still love this book and have faith in it. Next, I attend one of those writers' conferences that seem like they should be held at an airport Sheraton. It's at the Portland Airport Sheraton and they charge $50 a pop to sit down with literary agents. I am working a temp job and only have enough cash to meet two.

I pitch the book to one agent solo and another in a chaotic group setting.

When Mary, the one-on-one agent, shoots me an email saying she'd love to represent me and doesn't even need to finish reading the manuscript, I—big shock—leave work early to celebrate. What a step forward! What a victory!

But it's more like literary hay fever. It keeps me from smelling the rotten eggs.

While Mary is enthusiastic about *Broken Piano for President*, I discreetly ignore red flags big enough to be seen from space. Such as: she's never sold a book and her résumé highlights include appearing in a Beck's beer commercial directed by Ridley Scott. Such as: her office is in a modeling agency and Mary admits that she *sometimes* does weekend baby shoots to keep in good standing with the landlord. I also overlook the fact that her first suggestion is to get an 8x10 headshot because my black glasses have a "writerly" look.

The next several months are a tilt-a-whirl of failure. Harper Collins says no, Viking calls *Broken Piano for President* "nauseating," Ben Stiller's production company claims it is too dark, Adam Sandler's production company turns up its nose like the manuscript is made from Academy Awards or dignity.

Soon, it becomes clear Mary and I aren't destined for greater things. It also becomes clear she has probably missed her medication. My super-agent is eventually forced to move from her home because she never sold any books and, according to her math, claims it is all my fault because I didn't say thank you enough.

2008: On my own again, I begin working harder than all of the jobs I've been fired from combined. Not tough to do. I pitch the book to probably 100 more agents and indie presses. I consider getting one of those inspirational coffee mugs because encouragement isn't exactly falling from trees.

A friend of a friend has a book published through super indie, Akashic Books, and I beg for a contact. One editor, Aaron, is incredibly receptive. He sends the manuscript around to the other editors and gets mixed feedback. Akashic passes. However, Aaron gives me a bit of advice that greatly helps tighten the book's voice. Moral victory.

2009: Many, many more rejections follow.

Eraserhead Press has a questionnaire for people wanting to submit. I fill it out, citing my favorite writers and music and movies. I soon hear back from the publisher, Rose. I seem like the kind of person Eraserhead would like to work with based on my oddball tastes. I pitch her *Broken Piano for President* but Rose, too, avoids it like eye contact in the Men's Room. Eraserhead wants something around 100 pages from new authors. I submit a story collection, *Sex Dungeon for Sale!,* and they release it in the fall.

2010: Pleased with *Sex Dungeon's* sales, Eraserhead asks what else I have. I again pitch *Broken Piano for President* and mention a couple of other projects that were brewing during my previous years of spectacular failure. They claim to like *Broken Piano*, but are more interested in a country music/astrophysics comedy I've written called *Black Hole Blues*.

2011: *Black Hole Blues* is released via Eraserhead imprint Lazy Fascist, future home of Blake Butler, Sam Pink, Scott McClanahan, and a host of other excellently eclectic authors. My editor, Cameron, says he thinks the time is finally right for *Broken Piano for President*.

My vision goes black. I pass out atop a thick nest of rejection slips and form letters.

Later this year, our first child is also born.

2012: After six years, 25 drafts, two ulcers and approximately

300 rejections, *Broken Piano for President* is released. The minute I send in my final edits—over a half decade of work and failure—I run into the nursery for a job I'm actually pretty good at: helping our screaming infant fart.

Something tells me this isn't how DeLillo finished *Underworld.*

WHERE DO BLURBS COME FROM?

I never knew what they were called.

"You know, those quotey things on the front of books," I described them years ago.

Later, I learned they were called *blurbs*.

I lived and died by those blurbs back before Amazon and Goodreads. They helped me play detective and discover new writers.

Reading someone was a "revolutionary new voice" from a favorite author legitimized whatever tome the words were found on.

So, when preparing my second novel, *Broken Piano for President*, for release, I eagerly wanted such praise. I imagined a kid picking up my book and seeing a *New York Times* bestseller call me "the future of American literature," or "a dazzling wit," or at least, "not horrible in bed."

It's surprising, but for as many big-time quotey things floating around the world's books, they aren't exactly easy to secure. Even for the sexually above average. Slapping that praise on a book cover usually happens in one of three ways:

1: Aim high. Look up a favorite author or her agent and send an email asking to ship off an Advance Reader's Copy (Essentially a crappy, unedited version of your book, known as an ARC) for a possible blurb.

Most famous authors are crazy busy and get enough ARCs to build their kids a fortress. So, inevitably, months pass and you realize this bestseller has ignored you. Your feelings are hurt for about three days.

2: Ask your writer friends. Start with the most popular ones you sort-of-know and work your way down. If you are lucky they will likely read part of the book and light some blurbic fireworks in your honor. I have been very fortunate with this approach, though all ignore my prowess between the sheets.

[**NOTE:** There's a middle step where already famous writers ask their already famous friends. Jonathan Franzen probably gets his blurbs by simply asking Thomas Pynchon and Maya Angelou at Thursday night scrapbooking club.]

3: Dodge flying French toast while learning how fake TV really is and fall ass backward into a potential blurb.

See, *Broken Piano for President* involves, among other things, freeze-dried hamburgers, deep-fried hamburgers and a burger more addictive than meth. So, in addition to hounding my literary heroes, I also sent ARCs to twisted foodie guys like Anthony Bourdain, Morgan Spurlock and Alton Brown. The white whale on this gastronomic blurb hunt was gonzo chowdown king Adam Richman of *Man Vs. Food* fame.

Unlike the others, the jovial Richman was so difficult to track down I stopped believing he was real. The guy was probably just a CGI image. It made sense. How else could I explain someone wolfing down a 10 pound pizza without Pixar's help?

Try finding Richman online, I dare you. The guy has a thinner paper trail than most illegal aliens. Nowhere on the internet could I find an email address or physical address for the phantom Richman. Not an agent. Not a manager. Not even a cardiologist begging him to stop. [**Wentastic Fact:** This research did help me discover Richman's first televised eating challenge was The Big Texan!]

So, imagine my surprise when I found Adam Richman around the corner from my house in Louisville, KY—catapulting French toast through the air.

This neighborhood restaurant, Lynn's Paradise Café, is always on those travel-centric food shows because of its wacky décor, hour-long breakfast waits and $45 omelets. One Wednesday afternoon last summer I walked past its parking lot and saw a small crowd and a camera crew.

"*Man Vs. Food* is going to be shooting," one onlooker told me. "Adam Richman's here!"

"That CGI guy?" I said.

She squinted at me.

What luck! I quickly embedded myself into the crowd and waited to ask America's favorite overeater to pen a few sentences about my brilliance. Perhaps he's heard about my could-be-worseness in bed? Toss that in, too, please.

Man, was I glad I took that walk.

The crew rigged some wood and rubber band catapult system. The idea was to launch a slice of batter-dipped toast across the parking lot onto a hot griddle. After an hour in the burning Kentucky sun, a round man in shades and a grey shirt exited a trailer. I watched closely for that telltale digital flicker of holograms, but no, Richman was real!

Real boring, at that.

As previously mentioned, actual movies take forever, but I never knew TV took so long to shoot and reshoot and reshoot and reshoot. For every 10 seconds the elusive Adam spends onscreen, it's safe to say five minutes go into repeating the shot. It also looks like a hell of a lot more work than I figured.

Eventually, after failing to hit the griddle target, the crew simply faked the Apollo 11 of French toast and urged the crowd to pretend to go wild. Ahhh, TV magic.

Lunch break arrived and I was as pink and sweaty as Richman after conquering a nuclear hot wing contest. Adam walked by and I asked if he had a second. Behind sunglasses, he stared at me, like: "Oh, boy, another question about that ten pound pizza."

I told him my novel was about hamburgers more addictive than meth. I thought he'd find it funny. Could I send it to him for a possible blurb?

He looked at me like he wished I'd asked about pizza instead. "That's cool. I just wrote a book," he managed, vaguely distracted.

"Totally. I know!" I blurted before my mind could inform me that, no, I wasn't aware he'd written a book.

"Sure, yeah, send it to our production company," he said. "That's the one way I'll definitely see it."

An assistant gave me the address and I quickly mailed off an ARC with a very nice note.

Later, I discovered Richman isn't completely devoid of a paper trail. He's a prolific Tweeter, so I followed up a few weeks later on Twitter.

This was almost a year ago. The book already came out in March. I'm still waiting to hear back.

All this silence wouldn't be a problem if only I'd been accepted into that damn scrapbooking club. Jonathan Franzen's exclamation point-filled blurb about my iffy-at-best sexiness was *this* close.

Thankfully, I have generous writer friends who weren't too busy launching breakfast across parking lots to pen a quotey thing for me.

FROM STAG PRESTON TO SMOKING EYEBROWS: WHY ROCK NOVELS RARELY WORK

It usually goes like this:

1.   Rockstar is born not a rockstar, but to a dismal family of chicken farmers or garbage pickers or libertarians.

2.   Rockstar buys guitar and struggles. Suspiciously, Rockstar is surrounded by naysayers recommending more lucrative careers in livestock breeding or politics.

3.   Rockstar gets really freakin' good in a suspiciously short amount of time. Rockstar wins lots of fans. Naysayers turn to yaysayers.

4.   Rockstar meets drugs. Drugs meet rockstar. It's a match made in heaven until it's not anymore. Suddenly, the simple life of trash picking seems like a step up from this gutter.

5.   Rockstar finds redemption in the form of a woman, an estranged child, or Ron Paul.

This story arc is so easy. That ease is why there are a million rock 'n' roll novels. It's also why there are tons of *forgettable* rock novels.

I've interviewed hundreds of bands and once, even, toured with a group. I sold their t-shirts up and down the West Coast. In that time I learned touring rock bands are mostly boring. I also learned the above story arc is *never* the case. Thirdly, I learned musicians love cigarettes. Who knew?

My point is: most interesting music stories are never tied up with a neat, redemptive bow on the final page. If this were true, Keith Richards would be passing out Jehovah's Witness pamphlets a dozen times over. Good rock 'n' roll fiction avoids said arc like the rest of us avoid cutting in front of Axl Rose at the buffet.

When I began writing my novel, *Broken Piano for President*, six years ago, I worked extra hard to avoid the above cliché. Looking back, it's all thanks to noise bands.

I was, at the time, a rock critic with *Willamette Week* in Portland, OR. I mostly covered weird, avant garde, noisy music. After getting the scoop from outsider musicians and artists, I knew the standard rock book arc was about as realistic as a chicken farmer still owning enough fingers to even play a guitar.

Broken Piano for President is a comedy about the world's worst rock band, productive alcoholism, hamburgers more addictive than crystal meth and conspiracy theories involving cosmonauts. What those countless interviews taught me was that the element making a noise band so exciting is the same thing that makes a rock book exciting: the element of surprise. Both take known formulas and torque them until something memorable and wonderful comes out.

Here's a list of rock novels that got it right and avoided chicken farmerdom:

GREAT JONES STREET by Don DeLillo.
This is my favorite rock book. Supposedly based on Dylan's frequent slips from the spotlight, DeLillo's Bucky Wunderlick is a mega-star-cum-NYC-Squatter just looking for some peace and quiet. However, it's not going to happen as hangers-on, managers, and a commune selling a super drug all tug at Bucky's jacket fringes. Like most of DeLillo's work, it nails America's invasive culture perfectly without soaking the specifics in highlighter pen.

In addition, this is DeLillo's most solid pre-*White Noise* book.

I AM STILL THE GREATEST SAYS JOHNNY ANGELO by Nick Cohn.
I'm always surprised so few people know about *I Am Still The*

Greatest... One of the earliest entries in the rock novel canon, Cohn's Johnny Angelo rises from the muck to ridiculous, cult-like heights. This 1968 book finds little to no redemption in seeking out one's artistic vision. It only offers trouble and pain and wonderfully black humor.

Even more incredible is the fact that Cohn, who's gone on to a stellar career as a rock critic, was 19 when he wrote it. Supposedly, Angelo was based on the destructive Texan/Brit pop star, PJ Proby. Though, the darkness of the novel seems like it's what could've happened if Scott Walker set his sights on conquering the teen pop market instead of singing tunes so dark they make Ingmar Bergman films feel like *Kindergarten Cop*.

SPIDER KISS by Harlan Ellison.
After an exhausting couple seconds on Google, I've determined this is the original rock novel. Written in 1961, Ellison's story follows the typical phoenix flight of Stag Preston to roots rock stardom. Based heavily on Elvis and Jerry Lee Lewis, the book eclipses those troubled singers' tar blackest moments and rapidly unravels into a horrific mess.

It's tough to tell if Ellison (best known for his sci-fi work and general assholery) loved or hated rock music at the time of this book. It summersaults our innocent vision of the bobby socks era into its own special circle of Hell. While you know it'll end badly, it's impossible to stop reading *Spider Kiss*.

THE ANOMALIES by Joey Goebel.
Picture it: a Wes Anderson movie about rock bands set in rural Kentucky. Goebel's debut contains a wild cast of characters comprising the band, The Anomalies, including wheelchaired Satanists, geriatrics, little girls and Iraqi soldiers. What makes this book work is the heart with which Goebel draws them.

While it follows the above rock arc pretty close, you get the sense that Goebel owns that map and simply splices it to his liking.

ARTIFICIAL LIGHT by James Greer.
Easily one of the weirdest and most challenging rock books ever written. Greer, who was also the bassist for lo-fi rock gods Guided

by Voices, crafts a dense story around mid-90s Dayton, OH. Indie rock geeks will rejoice in spotting the references to Guided by Voices' inebriated singer Bob Pollard, alt-rock goddesses the Breeders, Brainiac and Swearing at Motorists—all bands that helped Dayton look like the new Seattle for a flicker of time. (I went to college in Dayton then, so I am one of those geeks.)

The story is told through the eyes of a librarian wading through the diaries of a Kurt Cobain-esque recluse who returned to his hometown, Dayton. Within, is the story of the singer, the strange lives of the Wright Brothers and, maybe, the meaning of life.

HAUNTED HILLBILLY by Derek McCormack.

Okay, wait, *Artificial Light* isn't the weirdest rock novel. Well, maybe, considering *Haunted Hillbilly* is a country music novel. But you can't have rock without Hank Williams, who is the surreal protagonist of McCormack's wild ride. Here, we get a traditional up-from-nothing biopic arc, but retold with Seuss-like lyricism meeting brutal minimalism, all set in a 1950s Nashville plagued by a homoerotic vampire.

Nothing else reads like a Derek McCormack book. They rarely stack above 150 pages, but always manage to push boundaries thought impossible by raw words, queerness and even vampiric good taste. See his cartoonish old-timey music/funhouse novel *The Show That Smells* for further proof.

NEVER MIND THE POLLACKS by Neal Pollack

Probably the funniest rock novel ever written. Pollack lampoons pop music history and rock criticism by placing a character named "Neal Pollack" at the forefront of every major music movement known to man. *Never Mind* is a *Zelig* for record collectors and McSweeney's subscribers.

STONE ARABIA by Dana Spiotta

Come for the promise of Robert Pollard-like reclusive genius, stay for the soberingly articulate meditation on middle age and death. *Stone Arabia* centers around *The Chronicles*—a 30-year project by the main character's brother to record albums, make fake band histories and even write his own record reviews. *Arabia* proves light on *The*

Chronicles' compelling potential rabbit hole of musical fun, and gets heavy with thoughts on mortality. Somehow, it all works. Thanks, likely, in part to Spiotta's sharp prose.

THE GOSPEL SINGER by Harry Crews.
Again, not technically a rock novel. But, it's about gospel. And you can't get R&B without gospel. And rock would need Viagra without R&B.
So there.
Crews' punishingly weird South is at its finest in his debut. While everyone in the book is beyond emotional or societal repair, *The Gospel Singer* says a lot about the nature of celebrity. The musicians we worship aren't the people we think they are. But we feed off their magic all the same.
It's like saying you only think Bono spends his free time driving solar-powered cars and rescuing African villagers. If you don't assume he also manages to snooze in Tahitian hammocks and pilot diesel-guzzling yachts, I have a Rolex to sell you.
But still, we need a Bono. And the folks of Crews' Enigma, GA need The Gospel Singer. No matter what depths he sinks to.

LIFE by Keith Richards.
If this book is 100% nonfiction I will shave my eyebrows and smoke them. (I'm pretty sure Keith did the same on page 363). Two things are clear throughout this killer memoir: 1.) Richards has lived an insanely interesting life; 2.) Like most great oral storytellers, he is bullshitting the details to make a good yarn.
I'm okay with that, because the voice in this book is unlike anything I've ever read. Drug-tastic acrobatics, paling around with Jamaican warlords, Keith's taste in nautical literature—it's all there. Oh, also, he managed to write a bazillion amazing songs and dishes on their creation as casually as you and I brewing morning coffee.

BUY MY PAPERS, ITT TECH

TO:
Eugene Feichtner
President, ITT Technical Institute
13000 N. Meridian Street
Carmel, IN 46032-1404

Dear President Feichtner,

With the recent passing of author Harry Crews, I discovered that the University of Georgia Library purchased his collected papers in 2006. Soon, I learned that many writers' manuscripts, letters and doodles are frequently bought by colleges for scholarly research. For example, the University of Texas' library owns every scrap of Don DeLillo's filing cabinets. This led to asking the obvious: "Why not me?"

I am writing to offer ITT Technical Institute's library (you guys have a library, right?) exclusive rights to obtaining the Patrick Wensink Papers.

I'm prepared to clear out my office and deliver ITT my entire personal output for an undisclosed sum (papers seem to always sell for undisclosed sums. Let's shoot for that). This includes numerous manuscripts of all three of my books, a hard drive containing multiple electronic drafts of every novel, short story and essay I've ever penned. All of my notebooks, filled with regrettable book title ideas, like "Big Shadow Shits Little Shadow," and late-night epiphanies such as "Why aren't there more doo-wop groups in literature?" This deal also entitles ITT Tech to the entirety of my email correspondences (George Saunders once politely declined to blurb my book!).

Ah, but that's not all!

ITT students can learn about persistence from my numerous failures. Included in the Wensink Papers will be the hundreds of rejections my latest novel, *Broken Piano for President,* received, including one Viking Press editor who called it "Nauseating." As a special treat, I still have a few hate mails I got as a rock critic in Dayton, OH, stemming from a 2002 review claiming the new Trail of Dead album sucked.

Need more? Okay. I see Harry Crews' papers also consist of royalty statements. Consider it done! (This includes that dismal statement from June 2010 when I banked $3.63.)

Sounds pretty tempting, right? But you're thinking: *Why ITT Tech?*

True, I never attended your fine institute of higher learning. But Crews didn't go to Georgia, and I'm pretty sure Don DeLillo has never set foot outside the New York metropolitan area. So I think we're okay on that front. My papers will be a great learning tool for ITT academics. Students could write theses about me! I could come and speak to stenography classes on the importance of typing!

President Feichtner, you're probably also thinking: *Yeah, but those guys were all famous authors. You're no Don DeLillo, Mr. Wensink.*

Right again. But you're not exactly Harvard.

Or even Middle Tennessee State, for that matter.

That's why we're perfect for each other! ITT is America's third most-popular degree mill and I'm America's 103rd most-popular humorist (right behind Dane Cook).

You're looking at the ITT Tech of humor writers.

Plus, I might still get famous. It could happen. My chances of publishing a Pulitzer-winning novel might be slim, but my likelihood of gaining notoriety by impregnating Snooki or falling down a well are astronomically high (I drink a lot). When that happens, owning The Wensink Archive will be a terrific boon for ITT Tech.

And, because of this kinship, the Patrick Wensink Papers are offered at a bargain rate. Crews, DeLillo and the like sold their papers when they were well-respected pillars of literature, probably for hundreds of thousands of dollars (T.C. Boyle's papers just sold for a whopping $425,000). My literary estate can be yours for an undisclosed sum that hovers right around the price of a club sandwich and a Dr. Pepper.

Please keep in mind that I could have taken this juicy, once-in-a-lifetime educational offer to those jokers at DeVry or the University of Phoenix. But I chose ITT Tech, Mr. Feichtner. I am soliciting you and your institute because of your relentless dedication to the student body and the paralegal arts.

I look forward to hearing your thoughts on ITT Technical Institute acquiring the Patrick Wensink Archive. I am willing to meet at any of your 140 campuses. Frankly, the sooner the better. My wife is pretty pissed about how messy my office has become. So, ITT would, obviously, be doing me a solid.

Best,
Patrick Wensink
America's 103rd Most-Popular Humorist

MI SHITHOLE ES SU SHITHOLE

My office is a shithole.

Or so my wife tells me a couple times a week.

To me, it's not so much a shithole as a meticulously managed chaos all neatly packed within square footage smaller than most bathrooms. And for reasons that would require a large therapy bill, this cyclone of crap is the only place I can focus.

A quick survey of this room finds:

- A half-bag of confetti.

- Dozens of crumpled pastel Post-its (Featuring such stumble-drunk bits of wisdom as "There is a loop and I am out of it" and "What would peanut butter and jelly say if it could talk?").

- A plastic tiger mask.

- Crumbs.

- A rumpled souvenir flag from Turks and Caicos.

- An *On the Road with Charles Kuralt* DVD.

- A seafoam green suitcase filled with an ancient 4-track recorder. Plus, dozens of tapes that I don't have the heart to throw away from back when I was in unknown bands like Clap Amp and Static Magic.

- A fantasy football trophy I was supposed to pass on several years ago (my team, the Unicornholes, was something like the 2009 champions).

• Crumbs.

• Easily 1000 CDs (I was a rock critic for many years). All of which I have listened to.

• Hundreds of books. Maybe half of which I've actually read. (Just stacked on my desk, we have *Roget's Thesaurus*, J.A. Tyler's *A Shiny, Unused Heart*, Tim Kinsella's *Karaoke Singer's Guide to Self Defense*, Evelyn Waugh's *Scoop* and John Le Carre's *The Spy Who Came in From the Cold*.)

• A broken DVD player.

• Some contraption called "The One-Armed Boozer," which was some 1970s gag gift that converts a liquor bottle into a slot machine that doles out shots. My friend, Lydia, gave it to me as a gift years ago.

• More crumbs.

• An enormous cardboard poster of Sting encouraging literacy.

I purchased that ridiculous Sting poster at a Dayton, OH library sale in 2002. It was the first thing I bought after graduation and finally being on my own. I actually debated whether to get it because it was childish and I would soon be getting a career and growing up.

It's cute how naïve I once was.

Sting is the centerpiece of the room. The poster features the man born Gordon Sumner, wearing some frilly costume leftover from *Game of Thrones*, reading a book next to…a castle. Nice work, Sting. It's not like reading doesn't already have a pretentious reputation amongst America's youth.

During my decade of Sting-ownership, especially the past six years, he's helped me write. I never got that career, so I kept Sting and started writing books instead. "READ" say enormous blue letters above the Brit's bleach blonde mane. The poster has hung in every pseudo-office I've ever scraped together since beginning my first novel in Portland, OR in 2006. From that crumbling duplex, to that house with no heating where I wore a winter coat while typing, to that walk-in closet, to my current shithole in Louisville, KY…Sting's always looking over my shoulder, forcing his taste in Charles Dickens down my throat.

And Sting will stay if this cleaning lady's nightmare of an office ever moves again. In some weird way, Sting equals motivation. Not because his lacy cuffs and collar promise a whimsical world hidden within literature, but because he sucks so badly. (Remember, I was a rock critic. "Sting Sucks" is embossed on the back of our business cards. Union rules.)

I was born to do the exact opposite of what Sting asks. If he sings, "If I Ever Lose My Faith in You," I lose faith faster and change the station.

When the king of new age prisses—a man who once titled an album *The Dream of the Blue Turtles* for God's sake—urges me to donate to UNICEF, I find a Filipino sweatshop to invest in.

Whenever the former Police frontman tells me, "READ," I defy him. Instead, I force myself to "Write."

My books usually go through about 25 revisions during their lifespan. And as the garbage piles higher in my office, those novels get better. I'd like to think if Sting and his smug face weren't watching, I might have given up, or worse listened to his music. Instead, I penned some books I'm very proud of, concerning such un-Stingly topics as productive alcoholism, noise rock bands, hamburgers more addictive than meth and cosmonauts.

Sting, you might have just earned yourself a half-bag of confetti to say, "thank you." Watch your mailbox.

I WAS (INTERNET) FAMOUS
FOR FOUR DAYS

For less than one week, I was famous. Famous enough that the employees at my optometrist's recognized me. But not famous enough to get free glasses.

In other words, internet famous.

I'm not complaining. I'm just saying, it's not Harrison Ford notoriety. It's Star Wars Kid fame. And now, for the most part, it's gone.

Here's a look inside the viral meme hurricane.

FRIDAY, July 19
A week earlier, Jack Daniel's sent me a very polite cease and desist letter claiming my novel's cover (*Broken Piano for President*) infringed upon their trademark. My publisher decided to change the cover art.

I post the letter on my blog, calling it
"The World's Nicest Cease and Desist."

Amazon Sales Rank: **500,000ish**

SUNDAY, July 22
Esoteric news source BoingBoing runs a brief bit on the Jack Daniel's letter. Later in the day, Mashable picks it up.

Shockingly, the book enters Amazon's Top 1,000 sellers: a huge accomplishment for a small, independent book. My editor, Cameron Pierce, and I frantically begin sending emails, assuming, at any moment the book will plunge back into obscurity.

Amazon Sales Rank: At one point the book slid from **509th** bestseller to **554th**. (*Cameron and I decide our moment has passed and that this is already an amazing accomplishment.*)

MONDAY, July 23

I wake up to the book being the 154th bestselling title on Amazon. Ranked #1 in Satire, ahead of hacks like Kurt Vonnegut and Joseph Heller. My head is beyond spinning. I can't stop saying, "Holy shit, holy shit, holy shit" in disbelief.

I am rushed into my local NPR station for an interview and am pleased because a couple of elderly people might hear about me. By the time I get home from the interview, *The Atlantic* has picked it up. From there, things start reaching Overlook Hotel levels of craziness. Biggest of all, I suddenly have an Amazon Bestseller. 69th most popular book in all of America!

Non arts-based outlets pick up on the story, too, like those saucy sources of gossip: *Business Week* and *Intellectual Arts Management* magazine.

By mid-afternoon I make this Facebook post with all seriousness, because there is no way my little book can maintain this momentum: "Broken Piano is now #54 on Amazon. Right behind that book about that kid who died and saw heaven."

So...I guess I know what I need to do next.

I am compulsively checking Amazon, not to see if the book has risen any higher, but because I expect it to drop. I'm mentally telling myself: "Wow. It was a good time while it lasted."

A law school in Ohio asks me to come speak about trademark laws. Things will never be this weird again.

Late in the evening, mega news source, *The Huffington Post*, runs a story which is improbable enough. When they ask me to start blogging for them, I suffer my 15th heart attack of the day.

Amazon Sales Rank: **#32**

TUESDAY, July 24

I've never made many correct decisions in the publishing world, but posting my cease and desist goes down as the best move I've ever made. Before that, on a good day, my blog saw 20 visitors.

Since Sunday, I've seen over 150,000.

Today, things get wild in a hurry. The Jack Daniel's story appears in articles in Germany, Spain, France and more. My book's cover is on the front page of Yahoo!, of course, behind headlines like: "Mystery of 'Goat Man' in Utah Hills Solved."

My editor and I attempt to start a Twitter campaign to land me on the satirical news program, *The Colbert Report*. Anything is possible after the book is featured in *TIME* magazine.

I find myself punctuating most of my Tweets and Facebook posts with "!?!?!?!" because I know no other way to describe the mix of raw excitement and complete disbelief in my situation.

Then the book jumps to #9. Keyboards don't have enough exclamation points and question marks to describe the shock.

Amazon Sales Rank: **#9**

WEDNESDAY, July 25

I don't think it could get better than the *New York Times* writing an article, but then *The New Yorker* pens one sentence with my name in it. One sentence in *The New Yorker* is enough to call a career.

I decide to spoil myself. Gold watch? Tahitian vacation? Not quite. I purchase a $45 copy of Harry Crews' long out of print *Naked in Garden Hills*. Having never paid more than $15 for a book in my life, I instantly feel guilty.

In two short hours, I record a Skype interview for an online news program, answer questions from the *Telegraph (UK)* and a French magazine, then accept an invite to one of the biggest radio shows in America, NPR's *Weekend Edition*.

I have never been busier in my life and it is a joyful busy. The book is holding at #6 and is the bestselling Humor and Satire title amongst the millions of other books. Including *Everybody Poops*.

Amazon Sales Rank: **#6**

THURSDAY, July 26

I am greeted in the morning to a meaty piece of *Forbes Magazine* dedicated to my story. Somewhere, Donald Trump might be reading this while crushing someone's dreams.

I do more interviews, but not as many. The book begins to slide backward, first to a still-incredible #9 and eventually to #13, which still means two-jillion people are discovering *Broken Piano for President*.

There is a sense that I've seen the top of the mountain. I write my editor, telling him how everything feels like coming home from a long vacation. My surroundings are the same, but everything holds a strange emptiness waiting to be refilled.

I felt like the most popular man on Earth for four days and don't know how to downshift.

Amazon Sales Rank: **#13**

FRIDAY, July 27

To say that it's funny to be disappointed that one is only covered by the American Bar Association's magazine is a lesson in skewed perspectives. It's like Hugh Heffner getting grumpy because he only slept with three Playmates today.

The Amazon ranking continues to slide to respectable numbers. Eventually dipping out of the Top 100.

Colbert Report isn't calling.

The story has, apparently, reached a saturation point online. Everyone who knows about it knows about it. A quiet lull overpowers my jumbled mind. I think about calling the Star Wars Kid to see if he wants to hang out.

My Internet fame is officially over.

I took this week off from my job as a freelance writer and I will now return next week. Thank God I didn't buy that Tahitian island.

"!?!?!?!?!??!" gets packed away like a souvenir. A souvenir I am incredibly fortunate to own.

DIAPERS DO NOT WAIT FOR YAHOO! NEWS

Yahoo! News, one of the biggest media outlets on the planet, emailed me and asked me to do a Skype interview for their hugely influential *Trending Now* program. Hundreds of thousands of people would see this story. It was the kind of break an independent press author like me dreams of.

"Absolutely!" I said. "But can it wait an hour until naptime?"

Such was my day.

My novel, *Broken Piano for President*, was riding an insane wave of goodwill and popularity after the media picked up on the world's most polite cease and desist letter sent by Jack Daniel's whiskey. *Broken Piano's* cover parodied that famous black and white label. Usually, this is the part of a story where a lawyerly hammer crashes down hard. But not in my case. Jack Daniel's lawyers said they were "flattered" by the cover, but my publisher still had to get rid of it. However, Gentleman Jack was so nice, they offered to help pay for a new one! Unheard of kindness.

I declined their offer for money, but agreed to change the cover. From there, everyone from *Esquire* to *TIME* to the *New York Times* picked up the story. The novel rocketed to Amazon's Top 10 bestseller list in two days.

I should have been doing cartwheels. Years of hard work and suffering obscurity were finally paying off! I should have been running around the backyard and lighting Roman Candles. Naked. I should have at least been uncorking champagne, but my son was teething.

My boy, Walter, is nine months old and before walking ass-backward into the indie book media frenzy of the year, I was primarily a stay-at-home-dad. Those duties, I quickly learned, don't stop when Yahoo! News calls.

It never failed: if my editor phoned, ecstatic about *Forbes* covering our story, my son had a toxically dirty diaper in need of changing. While opening email, learning I was the Chuck Yeager of small press books, effectively breaking the sound barrier of Amazon's Top 10 sellers, I was also trying to distract Walter from gnawing through my computer cable with his four teeth. I came *this close* to hauling him into NPR's studio one morning until I found a last-minute babysitter.

Whenever a career high hit, there was a sobering slug of reality close behind.

And I wouldn't have had it any other way. Walter and I spend nearly 12 hours a day together, alone. Every day. We are best friends because, well, we have to be. Would you want to spend upwards of 40 hours a week with someone you hate? No, thanks. That's what office jobs are for.

I've always known family is there to pick you up when you're down. However, I didn't realize how valuable family was for keeping you in check until that time. Baby Walter made sure I wasn't shopping for Rolls-Royces, but that also meant he wasn't getting that solid-gold pacifier he's been going on and on about. Around our house, things will stay the same because family doesn't change when the news comes calling.

ACKNOWLEDGMENTS

A huge thanks to all the publications that printed many of these essays:

The Huffington Post
Thought Catalog
Metazen
The Fanzine
The Magazine of Bizarro Fiction
Smalldoggies
We Who Are About to Die
Fathermucker.com
Three Guys, One Book
The Next Best Book
Experiments in Manhood

Another round of thank yous to those on my email list who encouraged me, saying I should do "something" with all these weird stories from Portland.

ABOUT THE AUTHOR

Patrick Wensink is also the author of three works of fiction, including the international bestseller, *Broken Piano for President*.

He lives in Louisville, KY with his wife and son. You may have heard something about them.

Discover everything Wentastic: www.patrickwensink.com

WANT MORE INDEPENDENT LITERATURE?

Lazy Fascist Press recommends Future Tense Books. For over twenty years, Future Tense has been publishing top-notch fiction, poetry, and essays, earning a reputation as one of the leading independent publishers not only in Portland, Oregon, but in the entire country. We fully endorse the following Future Tense titles:

Everything Was Fine Until Whatever by Chelsea Martin

My Beloved 26th by Riley Michael Parker

OK, Goodnight by Zachary Schomburg and Emily Kendal Frey

Legs Get Led Astray by Chloe Caldwell

Partial List of People to Bleach by Gary Lutz

Double Header by Suzanne Burns

Before You She Was a Pit Bull by Elizabeth Ellen

To order any of these books, or for more information about Future Tense Books, visit www.futuretensebooks.com.

LAZY FACIST PRESS:
SUPPORTERS OF INDEPENDENT BOOKS
SINCE BEFORE THE APOCALYPSE

LAZY FACIST PRESS
2012

*9 7 8 1 6 2 1 0 5 0 6 4 3 *